BIBLE KEY WORDS

VOLUME V

Previously Published:

BIBLE KEY WORDS—Volume I

four books in one:
I. LOVE *by* Gottfried Quell
    and Ethelbert Stauffer
II. THE CHURCH *by* Karl Ludwig Schmidt
III. SIN *by* Gottfried Quell, Georg Bertram,
    Gustav Stählin *and* Walter Grundmann
IV. RIGHTEOUSNESS *by* Gottfried Quell
    and Gottlob Schrenk

BIBLE KEY WORDS—Volume II

four books in one:
I. LORD *by* Werner Foerster *and* Gottfried Quell
II. GNOSIS *by* Rudolf Bultmann
III. BASILEIA *by* K. L. Schmidt, H. Kleinknecht,
    K. G. Kuhn *and* Gerhard von Rad
IV. APOSTLESHIP *by* Karl Heinrich Rengstorf

BIBLE KEY WORDS—Volume III

two books in one:
I. FAITH *by* Rudolf Bultmann *and* Artur Weiser
II. SPIRIT OF GOD *by* Eduard Schweizer *and others*

BIBLE KEY WORDS—Volume IV

two books in one:
I. LAW *by* Hermann Kleinknecht *and* W. Gutbrod
II. WRATH *by* Herman Kleinknecht, J. Fichtner,
    G. Stählin, *and others*

BIBLE KEY WORDS

Volume V

from GERHARD KITTEL'S

THEOLOGISCHES WÖRTERBUCH
ZUM NEUEN TESTAMENT

A ONE-VOLUME EDITION CONTAINING
TWO BOOKS:

I. HOPE

by Rudolf Bultmann *and* Karl Heinrich Rengstorf

II. LIFE AND DEATH

by Rudolph Bultmann *with contributions by*
G. von Rad *and* G. Bertram

HARPER & ROW, PUBLISHERS
New York and Evanston

I

HOPE

BY

RUDOLF BULTMANN
and KARL HEINRICH RENGSTORF

Translated from the German by Dorothea M. Barton
Edited by P.R. Ackroyd

EDITOR'S PREFACE

THIS book is a translation of the article 'Ελπίς, written by Professors Rudolf Bultmann and Karl Heinrich Rengstorf in the *Theologisches Wörterbuch zum Neuen Testament* (TWNT), begun by G. Kittel and now edited by G. Friedrich, Vol. II, pp. 515-31. Apart from some curtailing of footnotes, the whole text of this short article is here translated and follows the order of the original. At the beginning of Chapter II a short addition has been made in the form of a list of the Hebrew words used in the Old Testament, to provide the basic information for the discussion which then follows.

The book traces the Greek usage of ἐλπίς with its predominantly neutral sense of 'expectation', and shows how it then does duty for the Old Testament terms in which anticipation of good or evil make for a feeling of hope or anxiety. Considerable space is devoted to the study of the development of the Messianic hope and to Rabbinic ideas, alongside those of the early church in which hope in God is in the Pauline literature a particularly important concomitant of faith. It is this Godward direction of hope—both in the Old Testament and in the New—which marks it off from any mere forethought or calculation of the future. In Chapter III the discussion of the Rabbinic material leads to the problem of the assurance of salvation, a problem which must be a pressing one in any religion which lays stress upon human obedience. That the problem is one with which Christians are concerned too is clear from the great deal of discussion which there has been at various times about assurance. The Christian's assurance rests in God and not in himself. But this means that it is not susceptible of exact demonstration, and that there must always remain in Christian thinking an element of the kind of agnosticism which recognises that it is improper so to reckon upon God's saving power as to make of Him less than He is—a means to an end.

The publication of the volume means that the triad *Faith*, *Hope* and *Love* is now complete. Cross-reference to the other two volumes has been made at one or two obvious points, but it is clear that the three concepts belong so closely together in Christian thinking that the discussion of any one of them must inevitably evoke the others, and the reader will frequently observe how nearly the terms overlap within the richness of New Testament thought.

All Hebrew words have been transliterated and, where necessary, translated. Greek words are not transliterated. Where quotations are given from elsewhere than the New Testament (or Septuagint), a translation has been given, except where the meaning is evident or where the actual Greek word used is of particular importance. In a number of cases translations have been given of crucial Greek words, but these are to be taken only as rough guides to the meaning, since, as will appear from their contents, these are words which are deserving of full and separate study. Such of them as appear in the New Testament are, of course, so treated in other volumes of TWNT.

Biblical references follow the normal chapter and verse enumeration of the Hebrew and Greek texts, with a note of deviations in the English versions. References to the Septuagint therefore in some cases require modification, particularly in the Psalter and in the book of Jeremiah.

CONTENTS

BIBLIOGRAPHY

STOBAEUS: *Eclogae* IV.997-1007.
TH. BIRT: *Elpides* (1881).
L. SCHMIDT: *Die Ethik der alten Griechen*, II (1882), pp. 69-74.
H. DE GUIBERT: *Recherches de Science Religieuse*, 4 (1913), pp. 565-596.
A. POTT: *Das Hoffen im NT* (1915).
F. WEHRLI: *ΛΑΘΕ ΒΙΩΣΑΣ* (1931), pp. 6 ff.
A. LESKI: *Gnomon*, 9 (1933), pp. 173 ff.

CHAPTER III

H. L. STRACK and P. BILLERBECK: *Kommentar zum NT aus Talmud und Midrasch*, I-V (²1956), see III, pp. 217 ff.
Jewish Encyclopaedia, VI, pp. 459 f.
G. F. MOORE: *Judaism*, I-III (1927-30), see II, pp. 287 ff.
W. BOUSSET: *Die Religion des Judentums im späthellenistischen Zeitalter*, ed. by H. Gressmann (³1926), see index under 'Hoffnung'.
G. KITTEL: *Die Religionsgeschichte und das Urchristentum* (1932), pp. 130 ff.
E. STAUFFER: 'Paulus und Akiba. Der erlösende und der tragische Ausgang des Judentums', *Saat auf Hoffnung*, 69 (1932), pp. 113 ff.
W. WICHMANN: *Die Leidenstheologie* (1930).
S. MOWINCKEL: *He that cometh* (ET 1956).

Reference may also be made to the general theologies of the Old and New Testaments, and to A. Richardson, ed., *A Theological Word Book of the Bible* (1950), and J.-J. von Allmen, *Vocabulary of the Bible* (1958).

ABBREVIATIONS

Anth Pal   *Anthologia Palatina*, ed. Stadtmüller and Bucherer (1906).

BMI   *Collection of Ancient Greek Inscriptions in the British Museum* (1874 ff.).

Diels   H. Diels, *Die Fragmente der Vorsokratiker*, ed. W. Kranz (I, ⁷1954; II, III, ⁶1952); cf. K. Freeman, *Ancilla to the PreSocratic Philosophers. A complete translation of the fragments in Diels* . . . (1948).

Ditt Or   W. Dittenberger, *Orientis Graeci Inscriptiones Selectae*, I-II (1903-5).

Ditt Syll   W. Dittenberger, *Sylloge Inscriptionum Graecarum*, I-IV, 1, 2 (³1915-24).

Epigr Graec   *Epigrammata Graeca ex lapidis conlecta*, ed. Kaibel (1878).

ET   English translation.

EVV   English versions.

Pr-Bauer   E. Preuschen, *Griechisch-deutsches Wörterbuch* . . . *NT*, ed. W. Bauer (⁵1958). ET of ed. 4 (1949 ff.) by W. F. Arndt and F. W. Gingrich (1957).

Str-B   Strack-Billerbeck, cf. Bibliography.

Thes Steph   H. Stephanus, *Thesaurus Graecae Linguae* (1831 ff.).

TWNT   *Theologisches Wörterbuch zum Neuen Testament*, ed. G. Friedrich.

I. THE GREEK CONCEPT OF HOPE

1. *General usage.*

'*We are always filled with hopes all our lives.*' These words from Plato's *Philebus* 39e occur in an analysis in which he demonstrates how human existence is determined not only by the αἴσθησις (perception) which apprehends the present, but also by the μνήμη (memory) of the past and the expectation of what is to come[1]; in fact what happens is that both the remembrance of the past and the expectation of what is to come (προχαίρειν and προλυπεῖσθαι, 39d) are not based on objective judgement and calculation, but on an expectation for oneself, a fear or a hope, the content of which in each case grows out of what a man understands to be possible for himself. 'What a man is determines what he hopes and how he hopes.'[2] He whose hopes are real (ἀληθεῖς) is favoured by the gods (θεοφιλής). Expectations and hopes are the images which a man forms for himself of his future.

It is an attribute of human nature to have ἐλπίδες,[3] that is to say, to begin with: expectations of the future (ἐλπίς = προσδοκία[4]), happy ones and sad ones. What

---

[1] 'Ελπίς and μνήμη have a similar relationship in Aristot. *Metaph.* XI.7, p. 1072b, 18; *Rhet.* II.8, p. 1386a, 2 f., 30; *De Memoria* I, p. 449b, 10 ff.

[2] H. G. Gadamer, *Platos dialektische Ethik* (1931), p. 138; cf. the whole of his interpretation of *Philebus* 35a-41b on pp. 126-39.

[3] Stob. V.1001.13 f.; Eur. *Tro.* 632 f.; he who loves, hopes; Plat. *Phileb.* 39e; Theocr. 4.42; cf. Birt, *op. cit.*, pp. 6 ff.

[4] The examples in note 1 above show this; cf. Plat. *Phileb.* 36a ff.; ἐλπίς = anxious expectation, apprehension, e.g. Eur. *Iph. Aul.* 786. 'Ελπίζειν often means to believe, to suppose, e.g. Pind. fr. 61;

we mean by hope is called ἐλπὶς ἀγαθή,[1] even though later on ἐλπίς by itself is used with the meaning of hope,[2] in which the original etymological sense of the stem ἐλπ- is again brought out.[3] But the manner in which the fact that ἐλπίζειν is a component part of man's nature is interpreted on each occasion, is very significant for the Greek understanding of human existence. In Soph. Ant. 615 f. the equivocal value of ἐλπίς is expressed:

> To many hope may come in wanderings wild, a solace and
>   a joy
> To many, shows of fickle-hearted love.

Emped. fr. 11 (I.227.21 Diels); Heracl. fr. 27 (I.83.5 f. Diels); Aristoph. Av. 956. Παρ᾽ ἐλπίδα is often used as a synonym for παρὰ γνώμην (cf. TWNT I, p. 690, n. 7) cf. Soph. Ant. 330 f. Ἀνέλπιστος = 'unexpected', e.g. Eur. Iph. Taur. 1495; Hel. 412. Synonymous with ἀδόκητος, Hel. 656.

[1] Plat. Leg. I.644e. The nature of ἐλπίς is determined by attributes such as ἀγαθή (Pind. Isthm. 8.15; Plat. Leg. IV.718a; Aristot. De Virtutibus et Vitiis 8, p. 1251b, 34 f.; Ael. Arist. Or. Sacr. 48.28); καλή (Plut. De Bruto 40 [I.1002c]; Stob. I.403.21); γλυκεῖα (Pind. fr. 214; Plat. Resp. I.331a); ἱλαρά (Critias fr. 6 [II.315.11 Diels]); χρηστή (BMI 894, in P. Wendland, Die hellenistisch-römische Kultur [1912], p. 410; often in Philo); on the other hand as κακή (Plat. Resp. I.330a). Frequently the adjective εὔελπις (Plat. Ap. 41d; Phaed. 64a): to be εὔελπις is a typical quality of youth, in Aristot. Rhet. II.12, p. 1389a, 19 ff. The leading character in Aristoph. Av. is Εὐελπίδης 'Hope well'.

[2] Thus in Pseud.-Plat. Def. 418a ἐλπίς is defined as προσδοκία ἀγαθοῦ. This usage agrees with the contrast frequently made later between ἐλπίς and φόβος, Birt, op. cit., pp. 6 (and p. 97, n. 17), 46 f. —Later ἐλπίς (ἐλπίζειν) is occasionally used beside προσδοκία (προσδοκᾶν), see Preisigke, Wörterbuch der griech. Papyrusurkunden (1925 ff.).

[3] Ἐλπ-: an extension of the root vel (Latin vel-le) with p: as in Latin also in volup (voluptas); in Greek ἀλπ- in ἔπαλπνος 'desirable', ἀλπαλέος, ἀρπαλέος, ἄλπιστος, cf. A. Walde–J. Pokorny, Vergleichendes Wörterbuch der indo-germanischen Sprachen I (1930), p. 295.

It is a solace for man in the midst of present troubles that, or if, he may still hope, cf. Hom. *Od.* 16.101 and 19.84: *for there is yet room for hope.* Hope is 'golden' (Soph. *Oed. Tyr.* 158) and the soul is disheartened which lacks its accustomed confidence of hope (Aesch. *Ag.* 994; cf. 262).

Pind. fr. 214: *Sweet companion with him, to cheer his heart and nurse his old age, accompanieth Hope, who chiefly ruleth the changeful mind of mortals.*[1]

Pind. *Isthm.* 8.15: *It is meet for man to take to heart good hope.*[2]

According to Thuc. V.103 ἐλπίς is an abating of danger. It can comfort the individual when in distress (in Democr. fr. 287 [II.20.5 f. in Diels]). Hence the old fable[3] which tells how Zeus gave man a cask filled with all good things, but that man beguiled by curiosity

---

[1] Plato in *Resp.* I.331a quotes this verse with the remark: *But him who is conscious of no wrong that he has done a sweet hope ever attends and a goodly* . . . , whilst the wicked lives *with an evil hope*; cf. *Leg.* IV.718a concerning the upright man: Aristot. *De Virtutibus et Vitiis* 8, p. 1251b, 33 f.; Eur. *Hel.* 1031. Cf. the opposite in Democr. fr. 221 (II.105.10 f. in Diels). Thus in Hesiod *Op.* 498 ff. ἐλπίς tempts the work-shy man to make bad plans.

[2] cf. Soph. *Trach.* 25 f.; Eur. *Herc. Fur.* 105 f.

[3] The original meaning of the fable is obviously preserved in Babrius 58 (P. Friedländer, *Herakles* [1907], pp. 39 ff.); in Hes. *Op.* 94 ff. it is elaborated, but the meaning is disputed (H. Türck, *Pandora und Eva* [1931], pp. 15 ff.). The same idea occurs in Theognis 1135 f. although he is aware that hope is double edged. In later times cf. Max. Tyr. 29, 6 b/c. In Heracl. fr. 18 (I.81.16 f. in Diels) ἐλπίς seems to be considered as the suprarational power in invention. According to H. Fränkel (in Türck, *op. cit.*, p. 6) contrary to Diels: 'He who does not expect what is not to be expected (that which exceeds all expectations) will not discover what is undiscoverable (inconceivable) and inaccessible.' For the significance of ἐλπίς as the motive force of craftsmanship which leads to prosperity see Birt, *loc. cit.*

lifted the lid, so that all the good things escaped to the gods, and as the lid was slammed down ἐλπίς alone still remained captive and now consoles mankind. The same theme occurs in Aesch. *Prom.* 248 ff.; Prometheus boasts: *I caused mortals no longer to foresee their doom* and in reply to the question: *Of what sort was the cure thou didst find for this affliction?* he answers: *I caused blind hopes to dwell within their breasts.* Whereupon the chorus says: *A great boon was this thou gavest to mortals.*

But hope is easily led astray[1] and is dangerous. Only a god is not mistaken in his expectations,[2] the ἐλπίδες of man are unreliable.[3] Man must not aspire to the distant but to the familiar, he must seize what is at his feet.[4] 'Ελπίς which waits for what is uncertain is contrasted with modesty of forethought (Pind. *Olymp.* 7.44). By means of forethought (Pind. *Nem.* 11.46) man makes himself master of the future by basing his judgement on present circumstances and acting accordingly. Thucydides (II.62) contrasts *hope which is strongest in perplexity* with *reason, supported by the facts, which gives a surer insight*

---

[1] cf. Plat. *Tim.* 69d. The (θεὸς) ἐλπίς leads astray in Eur. *Iph. Taur.* 414 ff.; *Suppl.* 479 ff.

[2] Pind. *Pyth.* 2.49.

[3] Pind. *Olymp.* 12.5 f. (in general: 12.1-13 and *Pyth.* 10.59-64, 12.28-32); *Pyth.* 3.19-23. In *Nem.* 11.42-48 destiny directs the race of mortals, but our limbs are fettered by unfortunate hope; this wells up out of ἔρως, *desire* (cf. for this *Pyth.* 10.60; *Nem.* 3.30; Soph. *Ant.* 616; Plat. *Symp.* 193a). In *Isthm.* 2.43 the envious hopes hang round the souls of mortals. Cf. Solon fr. i.35 f. (Diehl). A hope is rarely fulfilled: Aesch. *Ag.* 505. Cf. Soph. fr. 205. In Soph. *Aj.* 477; cf. also e.g. Hes. *Op.* 498; M. Ant. 3.14; *Anth. Pal.* VII.376; for the opposite see πιστὸν ἔλπισμα in Epic. fr. 68 (Usener) (for this Plut. *Suav. Viv. Epic.* 6 [II.1090d]: πιστὴ ἐλπίς). Antiphon fr. 38 (II.303.2 f. Diels). For the relationship between hopes and dreams Birt, *op. cit.*, pp. 45 ff.

[4] Pind. *Pyth.* 3.20, 22, 60, 10.63; *Isthm.* 8.18.

into the future. This corresponds to the contrast in II.42 between ἐλπίς and ἔργον. In V.103 man goes astray if he takes refuge from his uncertain hopes in divination and the oracles.[1] According to Democritus the ἐλπίδες of fools cannot be realised; those of reasonable and educated men are better than the wealth of the uneducated (fr. 58 [II.120.20 f. Diels]); for the ἐλπίς of the clever man, which in that case is in fact no longer ἐλπίς in its original sense, is based not on τύχη (luck) but on φύσις (nature) which can be investigated scientifically.[2] The peculiarly Greek propensity to safeguard oneself against the future by intelligent adaptation to the order of the cosmos is expressed here in a characteristic way.

2. *Plato*

Plato indeed does not need to cut out ἔρως working effectively in ἐλπίς (cf. p. 4, n. 3), since he considers it to be the driving force towards the beautiful and the good. Therefore he can say of it in *Symp.* 193d: *Not only in the present does he (ἔρως) bestow the priceless boon of bringing us to our very own, but he also supplies this excellent hope for the future.* For Plato himself these *hopes for the future* already transcend the life of this world. When the darkness hides from man another better life, so that we being infatuated cling to the dubious glamour of earthly life (Eur. *Hipp.* 189 ff.), the philosopher is εὔελπις in face of death (Plat. *Ap.* 41c, *Phaed.* 64a). For he cherishes πολλὴ ἐλπίς that he will gain there *fully that which has been my chief object in my past life (Phaed.* 67b), and he

---

[1] cf. Aristot. *De Memoria* 1, p. 449b, 10 ff.
[2] cf. fr. 176 (II.96.12 ff. Diels). Cf. the contrary view in Heracl. (cf. p. 3, n. 3).

does not fear death (*Phaed.* 67c-68b), *for the prize is fair and the hope great* (114c). After all many have already even died of their own free will, supported by the hope that they will see again those of their own family who have preceded them in death (*Phaed.* 68a).[1] The mysteries which promise to their initiates a blessed life after their death[2] acquire increasing importance. Belief in the mysteries is also the reason why in Porphyry *Marc.* 24 ἐλπίς is reckoned with πίστις, ἀλήθεια and ἔρως as one of the four elements (στοιχεῖα) which make up real life[3]; however the desire and hope for ephemeral things must of course be cast aside (*op. cit.*, 29).[4]

3. *Hellenistic usage*

Of course earthly and human hopes also play their part in Hellenism beside hopes for the future.[5] Just as the gift of Zeus to mankind consists in his control of war and his bestowal of τύχη, ἐλπίς and εἰρήνη,[6] so too Augustus in the Priene Inscription is praised as the saviour who brings war to an end, fulfils old hopes and arouses fresh ones.[7] Stoicism devoted no attention to

---

[1] cf. *Life and Death*, to be published in this series.

[2] Isoc. 4.28, 8.34; Ael. Arist. 22.10. Cic. *De Legibus* II.14.36, *we have gained the power not only to live happily but also to die with a better hope.*—Cf. C. A. Lobeck, *Aglaophamus* (1829), pp. 69 ff.; E. Rohde, *Psyche* I (ed. 10, 1925), p. 290.

[3] The literature given in *Love* in this series, p. 59, n. 4. Porphyry describes in *op. cit.* how life is determined by the four elements. Cf. in addition Plut. *De Bruto* 40 (I.1002c).

[4] cf. in addition Jul. *Ep.* 89, p. 124.13, 139.2 f.

[5] For the role of ἐλπίς in the erotic literature see Birt, *op. cit.*, 3 f.; in the comedies and the Hellenistic and Latin literature influenced by it see Birt, *passim*; as an example especially Luc. *De Mercede Conductis.* Cf. also *Anth. Pal.* VI.330.1 f.; P. Oxy. VII.1070.10 f.

[6] cf. Stob. I 393.19 ff., 403.21.

[7] Ditt Or II.458 (in Wendland, *op. cit.*, pp. 409 f.). Similarly

the phenomenon of hope. In Epictetus ἐλπίζειν (ἐλπίς) is used with its early meaning of expecting.[1] He knows: *We ought to measure both the length of our stride, and the extent of our hope, by what is possible* (fr. 31); he emphasises: *We ought neither to fasten our ship to one small anchor nor our life to a single hope* (fr. 30); he exhorts, not *to look to others*, but *to hope from yourself* (III.26.11). Similarly Marc. Aur. Ant. exhorts: *Casting away all empty hopes, come to thine own rescue* (3.14).[2] The sentence of Epicurus is characteristic: *We must remember that the future is neither wholly ours nor wholly not ours, so that neither must we count upon it as quite certain to come nor despair of it as quite certain not to come* (Diog. L.X.127). In the *Anth. Pal.* IX.172.1: *neither hope nor good luck concerns me.*[3] Here it is taken for granted everywhere that ἐλπίς contains the image of a future devised from man himself.

in the inscription of Halicarnassus BMI 894 (cf. p. 2, n. 1); Ditt Syll³ 797.5 f.; Ditt Or 542.12, 669.7: ἐλπίζειν in the emperor (Galba); P. Oxy. VII.1021.5 ff. Cf. the inscription from Tomi lines 3 f., 34 f. published in the *Archaeol.-epigr. Mitteilungen* 14 (1891), pp. 22-26.

[1] I.20.13; II.20.37, 23.46; *Ench.* 40.
[2] cf. in addition for ἐλπίζειν 9.29, 10.36; for ἐλπίς 1.17, 5.8.
[3] Frequently ἐλπίς and τύχη are linked together, Birt, *op. cit.*, pp. 15 (p. 100, n. 57), 47, 91 (and 125, n. 215). *Spes et fortuna, valete*, is found in a Roman epigram on a tomb-stone. *Carmina Latina Epigraphica* (ed. Buecheler), 409.8.

II. THE CONCEPT OF HOPE IN THE OLD TESTAMENT

1. *Hebrew vocabulary and Septuagint renderings*

The OT uses the following words for *hope*: The commonest is the root *bāṭaḥ* (more than 100 times) and its derivatives *mibṭaḥ* (15), *beṭaḥ* (43), and also *biṭṭāḥōn*. The idea of *trust, security* is the most obvious here. Three other roots occur about 40 times each—*qāwāh, to wait* —and its derivative *tiqwāh, hope* (32); *ḥāsāh, to seek refuge*—and its derivative *maḥseh, refuge* (20); *yāḥal* (in pi'el and hiph'il, *to wait*—and its derivative *tōḥelet, hope* (6). Other words which occur seldom are: *sābar* (pi'el), *to hope, wait* (6); *sēber, hope*; *kesel, kislah, confidence* (5). The translations given here are only approximate and reference should be made to the discussion which follows.

The LXX as a rule renders *bāṭaḥ* and the nouns derived from it with ἐλπίζειν (ἐλπίς)[1]; yet for this group of words πεποιθέναι (πεποίθησις) often occurs. But πιστεύειν is never used. In addition, ἐλπίζειν stands twice for *qāwāh*, which is mostly rendered by ὑπομένειν (also ἀνα- and περι-), whilst ἐλπίς appears mainly for *tiqwāh* (only in Proverbs and Job and in addition in Ezek. xxxvii.11); πεποιθέναι (Isa. viii.17, xxxiii.2), προσδοκᾶν, ἐγγίζειν, ἐπέχειν are also used for *qāwāh*, ὑπόστασις and ὑπομονή for *tiqwāh*.

---

[1] Ἐλπίζειν occurs 47 times for *bāṭaḥ*, once for *beṭaḥ* (?); ἐλπίς too occurs 7 times for *bāṭaḥ*. In addition ἐλπίς is found 9 times for *mibṭaḥ*, 14 times for *beṭaḥ*, once for *biṭṭāḥōn*. On the breathing of ἐλπίς (ἐλπίζειν) see Thackeray, pp. 124 f.

'Ελπίζειν is put 20 times for *ḥāsāh* and 7 times for *maḥseh*; yet πεποιθέναι also stands 9 times for *ḥāsāh* and σκέπη, καταφυγή, βοηθός for *maḥseh*. The pi'el of *yāḥal* is rendered 10 times and its hiph'il 5 times by ἐλπίζειν; here too ὑπομένειν occurs beside it. *Tōḥelet* appears twice as ἐλπίς, once as ὑπόστασις, elsewhere other periphrases are met with.

Lastly *sābar* is rendered twice by ἐλπίζειν (twice by προσδοκᾶν); ἐλπίς is used once for *sēber* (so is προσδοκία once), once for *kesel*, once in a variant reading for *mabbāṭ* (Zech. ix.5 AQ). In addition there are odd cases: ἐλπίζειν for *dārash* (Isa. xi.10), *gālal* (Ps. xxii.9 [EVV 8, LXX xxi.9]), *ḥashaq* (Ps. xci.14 [LXX xc.14]), *shā'an* (II Chron. xiii.18), *shāqaq* (Isa. xxix.8), *rᵉḥaṣ* (Dan. iii.28), *nāsā' nephesh* (Jer. xliv.14) etc.; ἐλπίς for *ḥāzūt* (Isa. xxviii.18), *ḥesed* (II Chron. xxxv.26), *ṣᵉbī* (Isa. xxiv.16, xxviii.4 f.) *nāsā' nephesh* (Deut. xxiv.15); ἐλπὶς πονηρά for *zᵉwā'āh* (Isa. xxviii.19).

2. Old Testament usage

These facts are characteristic; they show that for the OT there is no neutral concept of ἐλπίς, which merely denotes expecting, so that an expectation would have to be qualified by the addition of good or bad as a hope or a fear. On the contrary to hope and to fear (with the future in view) are differentiated in the language from the first.[1] To hope, as the expectation of what is good, is closely connected with confidence, and the expectation means at the same time being eagerly on the look-out, in which the idea of patient waiting as well as that of seeking refuge may be emphasised.

[1] It is significant that where ἐλπὶς πονηρά occurs in the LXX (Isa. xxviii.19) it is a rendering of *zᵉwā'āh*, terror, horror.

Thus hope is always hoping for something good, and as long as a man lives, he hopes (Eccles. ix.4). But neither is such hope considered as a comforting fancy of the imagination, which may be forgotten in the distress of the present, nor is it a warning given against its uncertainty, as in the Greek world. On the contrary it is simply on hope that the life of the godly is fixed. To have hope and to have a future are an indication that a man is in a state of well-being.[1] Of course it is hope fixed on God.[2] Naturally this hope is primarily and normally expressed when a man finds himself in a distressing situation, out of which he hopes to be delivered and helped by God, and this hope is at the same time trust, so that *qāwāh* and *bāṭaḥ* appear side by side (Ps. xxv.1 ff.), or *qāwāh* occurs where otherwise *bāṭaḥ* is used in the same sense.[3] But this hopeful trust in God is

---

[1] Prov. xxiii.18, xxiv.14, xxvi.12; Job xi.18. If hope fails, then all is over, Lam. iii.18; Job vi.11, vii.6 *et passim*; the same is true of death, Isa. xxxviii.18; Ezek. xxxvii.4; Job xvii.15.

[2] He who trusts in God will receive help (Ps. xxvii.7), *will not be put to shame* (cf. TWNT I, p. 189, Ps. xxv.2 f., xxxi.6, 14, lxix.6, cxix.116; Isa. xlix.23). The fathers trusted in him and were not put to shame (Ps. xxii.4 f.). The godly trusts in God's *ḥesed* (Ps. xiii.5, xxxiii.18, 22, lii.9), *salvation* (*yᵉshū'āh*, Gen xlix.18; Ps. lxxviii.22), or *tᵉshū'āh* (Ps. cxix.81, 123 *et passim*); he waits upon God (Ps. xxv.21) and upon his judgement (Isa. xxvi.8); God is his refuge (Ps. ix.19 [EVV 18], lxv.5, lxxi.5, xci.9 [EVV 8] *et passim*). Blessed is the man who trusts in God (Jer. xvii.7; Ps. xl.5 [EVV 4], xci.1 ff.). The godly ought to trust in God and wait upon him (Ps. i.5, xxvii.14, xxxviii.3 *et passim*; Prov. xx.22, xxii.19 *et passim*); he confesses: I trust (trusted) in God (Isa. xii.2; Ps. xxv.2, xxviii.7, xxxi.7, 15 [EVV 6, 14], xci.2).

[3] *Qāwāh* in Isa. viii.17, xxv.9, xxvi.8; Ps. xxvii.14, xxxvii.9, lxix.7 (EVV 6) *et passim*. *Bāṭaḥ* in Isa. xxx.15; Ps. xiii.6 (EVV 5), xxii.5 f. (EVV 4 f.) *et passim*. Similarly *ḥāsāh* (Ps. v.12 [EVV 11], xvii.7), where otherwise *qāwāh* occurs (Isa. xl.31; Ps. xxxvii.9, lxix.7 [EVV 6]; Lam. iii.25); *mahseh* (Isa. xxviii.15; Ps. xiv.6,

demanded in every situation,[1] in the time of salvation as well.[2] Particularly when we reflect that the Psalms became the prayerbook of the community, it is clear that hopeful trust in God is demanded absolutely. The godly man knows that he always depends on what God will do, so that hope does not always expect something definite, does not fashion for itself a particular picture of the future, but consists in a quite general trust in God's protection and help.[3] Hence it can also be said that God is the hope, the confidence of the godly.[4] But in that case the Greek usage which contrasts ἐλπίς with what is at hand, with the familiar, or with foresight, anticipation on the basis of the available facts, is made impossible. The present too, which is thought by man to be at his disposal, is uncertain and cannot be turned to account. The distinction between hope and confi-

lxi.4 [EVV 3] et passim), where otherwise mibṭaḥ appears (Ps. xl.5 [EVV 4], lxv.6 [EVV 5]); in Ps. lxxi.5 tiqwāh and mibṭaḥ occur together; maḥseh follows in verse 7. In Jer. xvii.7 πεποιθέναι and ἐλπίζειν are both used as the rendering of bāṭaḥ and as that of ḥāsāh in Ps. lvii.2 (EVV 1); similarly in Isa. xxv.9 ἐλπίζειν and ὑπομένειν appear side by side for qāwāh.

[1] Jer. xvii.7; Ps. xl.5 (EVV 4), lii.9 (EVV 8), xci.2, cxii.7 et passim.   [2] Isa. xii.2.

[3] This is brought out with particular emphasis where it is said that God grants hope instead of help (Jer. xxix.11, xxxi.17; Hos. ii.17 [EVV 15]); similarly when the time of salvation is described as a time of confidence (Isa. xxxii.18; Ezek. xxviii.26, xxxiv.27 f.). But this is also expressed by the fact that in the statements concerning hope much less is said about what is hoped for than about the reason for hoping (God, God's faithfulness, God's name and the like). So ἐλπίζειν (ἐλπίς) ἐπί with the dative or accusative, εἰς, ἐν, which are uncommon or rare forms of expression in Greek, become frequent in the LXX. In Greek ἐλπίζειν with the dative means 'to rely on' (Thuc. III.97.2); ἐλπίδες εἰς occurs in Thuc. III.14.1.

[4] Jer. xvii.7; Ps. lxi.4 (EVV 3), lxxi.5.

dence disappears, i.e. confidence and certainty are
always at the same time a hope that the present situation will remain such that the factors on which one
relies will endure in the future. But when this hope is
not a hope in God, then all trust is an irresponsible
assurance which God will fearfully disrupt and turn
into dread and horror.[1] No one should trust in his
riches (Ps. lii.9 [EVV 7]; Job xxxi.24), in his righteousness (Ezek. xxxiii.13), in men (Jer. xvii.5), in his religious possessions, whether it be the temple (Jer. vii.4)
or Bethel (Jer. xlviii.13) or idols (Hab. ii.18). Men's
deliberations and calculations are a breath (Ps. xciv.11);
God brings them to nought (Ps. xxxiii.10; Isa. xix.3
etc.); *a man's mind plans his way, but the Lord directs his
steps* (Prov. xvi.9). The people and its calculating
politicians are put to shame when they build on the
resources of force at their disposal and on treaties with
foreign powers.[2] All such confidence imagines that it
can rely on what is at its command, but hope should
simply turn to Him who is not merely at one's disposal.
Such trustful hope in God is delivered from fear (Isa.
vii.4, xii.2; Ps. xlvi.3 [EVV 2]; Prov. xxviii.1); but it
must continue strictly hand in hand with the fear of God
(Isa. xxxii.11; Ps. xxxiii.18, xl.4 [EVV 3]; Prov. xiv.16,
26, xxiii.17). Therefore a man must be still and wait
upon God.[3] The antithesis is seen in Job who refuses
to wait (Job vi.11, xiii.15; cf. II Kings vi.33).

---

[1] Amos vi.1; Isa. xxxii.9-11; Zeph. ii.15; Prov. xiv.16. 'Care-
free' in a neutral sense, without any criticism expressed, in Judg.
xviii.7, 10, 27; Jer. xii.5; Job xl.23 (of the hippopotamus).

[2] Hos. x.13; Isa. xxxi.1; II Kings xviii.24; Isa. xxxvi.6, 9; Jer.
ii.37; Ezek. xxix.16.

[3] Isa. xxx.15; Ps. xxxvii.5-7, where *quietness*, or *being still* and
waiting patiently are combined with *bātah* etc.

Whilst at first God's help is expected to relieve actual trouble,[1] it is considered more and more to be the eschatological help which brings all troubles to an end.[2] The attitude of confident waiting and trustful hope develops more and more into the awareness that all earthly things and those of the present time are entirely temporary, and becomes the hope for the eschatological future.

[1] Ps. xiii.6, xxxiii.18, 22, cxix.81, 123 etc.
[2] Isa. xxv.9, xxvi.8, xxx.15, li.5; Jer. xxix.11, xxxi.16 f.; Mic. vii.7; Ps. xlvi.2 (EVV 1).

III. HOPE IN RABBINIC JUDAISM

1. *Linguistic evidence*

'Semitic had no strict equivalent for ἐλπίς.'[1] This remark indicates the linguistic situation for late Judaism in Palestine. There exists in fact no word which could be placed beside ἐλπίς as regards form and content. *Tiqwāh* has almost entirely disappeared[2] and the same is true of the rest of the OT words for which ἐλπίς and ἐλπίζειν appear in the LXX (cf. pp. 8 f). This is all the more striking, since it can by no means be said of the rabbinate that the concept of hope was alien to it. For this body in particular directed its thought very searchingly to the future; proof of this is already afforded by the mere existence of the Apocalypse of Baruch and of IV Ezra, which originated fairly certainly in the circles of the scribes in Palestine. Above all the messianic expectation occupied Palestinian Jewry and their leaders to an extraordinary extent during the first as well as during the second century of our era. In view of this attitude towards the future there must be special reasons for this lack of a word or a phrase defining it as a concept. These reasons can be found only in the particular nature of the future expectation of late rabbinic Judaism. Thus the recognition of the fact that an equivalent for ἐλπίς, ἐλπίζειν is lacking obliges us to analyse the content of the rabbinic expectation of the

---

[1] Schlatter, *Matt.*, p. 402.
[2] One of the exceptions is in Syr. Bar. lxxviii.6 where *tiqwat 'ōlām, eternal hope*, perhaps occurred in the Hebrew original (Wichmann, p. 39, n. 20).

future with a view to finding in it the explanation of the remarkable linguistic state of affairs.

2. *The messianic expectation*

(*a*) The messianic expectation for the future has a positive and a negative aspect. The positive aspect concerns the fulfilment of the hopes of Jewry; the negative one concerns the expectation of judgement which will come upon the ungodly at the dawn of the messianic age. For the latter, being enemies of God, are always also enemies of his people, and conversely by fighting against Jewry they incur the wrath and vengeance of its God. The two aspects of this expectation are intimately linked together, so that they can never be thought of separately, but always only in conjunction. In this context it is of no importance in what order the individual interventions connected with the dawn of the messianic era were expected and to what extent the group of conceptions was elaborated and constantly enlarged, especially with the help of the exegesis of scriptural passages.[1] The extensive complex of premonitory signs of the beginning of the messianic kingdom can also be left out of account here.[2] One point alone is of consequence, namely the fact that the messianic expectation is not a matter for the individual, but for the whole Jewish people and religious community. The individual has a share in it only in so far as he is a member and a part of this community; for the promises according to which the future will belong to God are given to Israel as a whole, and not to Israel as a collection of individual Israelites. Therefore only

---

[1] cf. the rabbinic material in Strack-Billerbeck, IV, pp. 857 ff.
[2] cf. Str-B. IV, pp. 977 ff.

that non-Jew can become a participant in the blessings
of the promises who has let himself be admitted by
circumcision[1] into the community of the Jewish people
and their religion as a member possessing full rights and
subject to full obligations.[2] But faith in the God of
Jewry does not by itself suffice for this[3]; on the contrary
it must be combined with the fulfilment of all the regu-
lations of the law as well. Amongst these the rule of
circumcision is not indeed put formally into the first
place, but yet from its nature it comes about that its
fulfilment is made to be the prerequisite of all other
real observance of the law.[4]

[1] For circumcision as the prerequisite of messianic salvation see
Str-B. IV, p. 40; as the reason for Israel's deliverance from Gehenna
see Str-B. III, p. 264, IV, pp. 1064 ff.

[2] The σεβόμενοι τὸν θεόν who are frequently mentioned in the
NT undertake only certain obligations (Sabbath, food rules), but
receive no rights, as is shown particularly by their relationship to
the temple and the sacrifices; here they are on exactly the same
legal footing as the pagans (Str-B. II, pp. 548 ff.). The rabbinate
seems all along to have been interested in the σεβόμενοι τὸν θεόν
only in so far as this 'status' contained the possibility of a gradual
transition to Judaism (cf. Juv. 14.96 ff. and the attitude of the
[Pharisaic: Str-B. I, p. 926] merchant Eleazar towards king Izates
of Adiabene: Jos. Ant. 20.17, 34 ff., especially 43 ff.).

[3] cf. for this simply the words of Eleazar to Izates (Jos. Ant.
20.44 ff.): *for thou oughtest not only to read them* (the Mosaic laws),
*but chiefly to practise what they enjoin thee. How long wilt thou continue
uncircumcised? but if thou hast not yet read the law about circumcision, and
dost not know how great impiety thou art guilty of by neglecting it, read
it now.*

[4] cf. Str-B. IV, p. 23. The comparatively rare mention in
rabbinic literature of the σεβόμενοι τὸν θεόν (Str-B. II, pp. 716,
719) may be in part at any rate connected with the fact that as the
actual piety of the law increased after the cessation of the cult due
to the destruction of the temple, Judaism came to reject more and
more a merely partial association, such as characterised this group.
The Jew who observes the law faithfully demands complete de-

Now the law is the determining factor for the relationship of the people to God. In it the Jews possess the unmistakable and complete revelation of the divine will. The work of the rabbis serves merely to elucidate it down to its smallest details and to work out all its refinements in order to enable Jewry to carry it out correctly in every particular. For God imparted his will to his people in order that it might be observed, but not in order to provide a consistent view of the world.[1] Since God's will does not change, just because it is God's will, and, moreover, because it is his will, it is always a will to save, the Judaism of the law expects that the coming age will have this in common with the present one, that above them both the law stands as the expression of the divine will. The difference between the two ages consists merely in the fact that the law is now entrusted to Jewry alone, whilst in the coming age the Gentiles too will observe it. This is an idea which occupied a large place, particularly in Hellenistic Jewry, and even determined its missionary work to a large extent[2]; but it was not alien to Palestinian Jewry. This is clear from their expectation that the messiah would teach the nations the law and make them subject to it.[3]

votion to it; and so long as this does not exist, he speaks of ἀσέβεια however great may be the leaning towards Judaism, and even if proofs of this are not lacking (cf. p. 16, n. 3).

[1] The rule that the study of the law is to be placed above its observance was first formulated in connexion with the persecution of Hadrian and the increasing difficulties imposed on religious practices by the edicts of the Roman government which was hostile to the law. For further details see Str-B. III, pp. 85 ff.; W. Bacher, *Die Agada der Tannaiten* I (1884), p. 303.

[2] Str-B. III, pp. 98 ff.

[3] cf. especially the Targum on Isa. liii.11, in which the *many* whom the messiah will subject to the law can only be non-Jewish

At the same time it is taken for granted that the messiah will expound the *torah* as no one else has done and that he will leave no doubt about its meaning, in so far as it is obscure or has been explained incorrectly till now.[1] It is also taken for granted that he will observe the *torah* in all its parts,[2] just as God himself also studies the law and keeps its precepts.[3] Since the observance of the law and the messianic expectation are thus bound up together, it is also natural to find that the rabbinate has made the dawn of the messianic era actually to depend on the perfect observance of the law by Israel. Thus according to a saying of R. Simon ben Jochai (c. A.D. 150) the salvation of Israel will begin as soon as the Israelites shall have kept the sabbath properly during the course of two sabbaths (B. Shab. 118b).

(*b*) This leads on to another fundamental factor in the messianic expectation. Its fulfilment does indeed lie in God's hand; but at the same time He has made it depend on the relationship of his people to Himself and to His will. This means that the dawn of the messianic era and of the messianic salvation is not merely God's doing. Man has a share in it and in fact in a

nations. The passages in Str-B. IV, p. 918 also assume that in the age to come the messiah will be actively engaged in teaching which is intended for all mankind. In so far as a difference exists between the expectation of Hellenistic and rabbinic Jewry, it lies only in the fact that the rabbinate, being conscious of its election, restricted its work in the main to the chosen people and attempted to prepare them here for the time of fulfilment.

[1] Str-B. IV, p. 1. Jesus links up with this conception of the new '*torah* of the messiah' by his exposition of the law in the sermon on the mount (Str-B. IV, pp. 1 ff.). Cf. also W. D. Davies, *Torah in the Messianic Age and the Age to Come* (JBL Monograph Series VII, 1952).

[2] Str-B. III, pp. 570 f.

[3] cf. Str-B. IV, pp. 1238 f. Cf. Index under 'God'.

quite decisive manner, namely in so far as it depends on his achievements when the Christ will come and bring in his kingdom. Thus the arrival of the messiah can be hastened, just as it can be delayed.[1] But thereby the messianic expectation of the rabbinate is subject to the same curse of uncertainty which afflicts the expectation of the future in every religion based on achievement. However certain a man may be that fulfilment will come one day, he is depressed by the knowledge that he is perhaps directly guilty of its delay, and it makes no difference whether it is to a greater or smaller extent. For after all there is no human yard-stick by which he might measure how far or how near he is to the goal. It is for God alone to decide this matter and His verdict lies in impenetrable darkness. This alone is certain, that God is absolutely just and that He will make no allowances for the people. In spite of all the ardour in the descriptions of what is to come, this introduces a certain element of weariness and particularly of uncertainty in the rabbinate's expectation of the end. This has been expressed in two ways—in the theory that the messiah is hidden, according to which he is already in existence and is only waiting for the moment of his coming forward,[2] and secondly in the endeavours to calculate in some way the hour of his appearance.[3] In both cases the attempt is made to overcome the uncertainty which arises from attaching the arrival of the messiah to the observance of the law by means of reducing the tension between this uncertainty and God's fixed plan. This has been proved to be the wrong way

[1] cf. for this the passages in Str-B. I, pp. 599 ff.
[2] cf. e.g. Str-B. III, p. 315.
[3] Str-B. IV, pp. 986 ff.

in both cases, since in each the human *ratio* forced its way into the foreground.

There is no more harrowing testimony to the correctness of this statement than that of Akiba who greeted Bar-cocheba as the Christ and thereby brought about the ruin of himself, of most of his pupils and to a large extent no doubt also of his people.[1] We possess a detailed account of his end at the hands of the Roman executioners (B. Ber. 61b). According to this he died with the words confessing the one God of the Jews (Deut. vi.4) on his lips; consequently he saw nothing discordant in placing his confession of God and his confession of Bar-cocheba side by side; on the contrary this action seemed to him to crown a life dedicated to God. It can be assumed that Bar-cocheba was still alive when Akiba died.[2] It is all the more impressive that in the hour of his death he was concerned only with his personal relationship to God, and not with the fate of the movement which by his share in it had brought about his condemnation to death. The text contains no suggestion that he had wavered. And yet his last words as recorded by it convey the impression almost of a self-justification before God; the speaker is dying for the sake of God in the service of his law, and not in service to the messiah. This reveals in a flash, as it were out of the subconscious, the uncertainty of the messianic expectation of the rabbinate. This appears also equally clearly in the fact that no rabbinic saying exists rejecting as presumptuous and mistaken Bar-cocheba's claim to be king, not even from the period long after he had

[1] cf. on this A. Schlatter, *Die Tage Trajans und Hadrians* (1897), pp. 50 ff.

[2] A. Schlatter, *op. cit.*, p. 52.

suffered a terrible end and had dragged Palestinian Jewry with him into destruction.[1] Although this fact implies in part a self-accusation by the rabbinate, yet it also reveals definitely how shaky the ground of the messianic expectation really was, even for those who in this matter had to appear as experts and were considered as such by themselves and by the people.

(c) But the attitude which all this demonstrates is something different from that which is meant by 'hope', even if the Greek word ἐλπίς is disregarded. Here it is always somehow a matter of calculation, made indeed from the human point of view, and it is by this means that the attempt is made to safeguard the expectation. This indicates the suppression of divine sovereignty in the sphere of the messianic hope, even if only in theory. It is therefore only appropriate that the NT should describe the pious Jewish circles at the time of Jesus who were gazing longingly into the future as προσδεχόμενοι (Mark xv.43 et passim) and not as ἐλπίζοντες. This word expresses assurance for the future combined with a consciousness of a rightful claim on the future. Even if it cannot be said that man's demands occupy the foreground, yet the emphasis is placed less on God's goodness, out of which future salvation arises and which can be grasped by faith alone, than on the existing promises which bind God to his people and to the fulfilment of its expectation. Here the question is not *how*, but *when*. Therefore the very nature of the rabbinate's messianic expectation made it impossible to conceive that it would take any other course than that of rejecting Jesus and his demand for faith. For the same reason Jesus' resurrection implied for the Jews the can-

---

[1] A. Schlatter, *op. cit.*, pp. 52 f.

cellation of their expectation and liberation for a hope which is a true hope because it is altogether bound up with God alone, and not with man.

(d) It is no doubt due to the special quality of the messianic hope and to the fact that in the last analysis it is no longer hope, that the idea of the *kingdom of heaven (malkūt shāmaim)* has to an increasing extent appeared beside it in Judaism. This appears as a particular entity, distinguished by being mainly concerned with the individual and by the possibility of its being realised. The dissociation in thought between the kingdom of the messiah before the end of the world and the kingdom of God at the last day exists in the meantime already in germ and is realised even now in the relationship of the godly man to God (cf. TWNT I, p. 572); it is also presupposed in the rabbinic apocalypses[1] and allusion is made to it by Paul in I Cor. xv.23; but it is based in the last analysis on the desire to overcome the hopelessness of the individual as a part of his people by making him himself the reason which sustains his hope. Thus the emphasis is of necessity laid upon his own achievements. But this means merely altering the formulation of the problem; it does not in fact solve it. Since the whole life of the godly in the present is determined by his view of the future, the assurance of his personal salvation now becomes the problem. Our sources show that here too the rabbinate failed to provide an answer.

3. *The problem of the assurance of salvation*

(a) Beside the messianic expectation shared by the

---

[1] cf. A. Schweitzer, *The Mysticism of Paul the Apostle* (1931, 1953), pp. 75 ff.

whole nation there stands the question of what the individual expects in the future. It concerns his portion in the world to come, which will be assigned in accordance with the decision taken by God Himself[1] when He separates the righteous from the ungodly and banishes the latter to Gehenna,[2] but bestows upon the former the joys of the Garden of Eden in the last days.[3] The decision is made by a forensic act. God ascertains on the basis of the law and of a man's achievements in accordance with it, just who can be regarded as righteous and who cannot be so regarded.[4] As the thought of his achievements has determined the life of the godly man in this age, so it also determines his eternal fate in the same way.

But this introduces into the hope of the individual members of the rabbinate the same element of uncertainty brought out in the analysis of the messianic hope as its most prominent characteristic. It is inherent in every religion based on achievement that its followers cannot reach any assurance whether or not they have obtained the required standard of pious achievement, since they are not acquainted with the rule to which they are subject.[5] This becomes evident in a particularly impressive way in the tenets of rabbinic Judaism, as one of the religions based on achievement, indeed as the classical one. Side by side with the assurance that God is keeping in readiness for the godly all the joys at His command, there stands the uncertainty whether a

[1] Str-B. IV, pp. 1100 ff.
[2] Str-B. IV, pp. 1106 f.
[3] Str-B. IV, pp. 1107 f.
[4] cf. e.g. J. AZ 2a, 14 ff. (Str-B. IV, p. 1203).
[5] B. Kid. 40a Bar. (Str-B. II, p. 427).

man's own achievement will after all suffice for him to
receive the blessing of salvation with the godly[1] and
whether it will not perhaps turn out in the end that
God's legal claim can simply never be fully met. This
lack of assurance of personal salvation[2] threw deep
shadows on the last hours of more than one of the great
teachers of Jewry. Rabban Johanan ben Zakkai, the
contemporary of the apostles,[3] wept when his disciples
approached his sick-bed to receive the last blessing of
their dying master; when they asked why he wept he
replied: 'Two paths are before me, the one leading to
the Garden of Eden, the other to Gehenna, and I do
not know along which path they[4] are taking me—why
then should I not weep?' (B. Ber. 28b). This is said by
the same man whom his disciples have just called 'the
shining light of Israel' and 'the strong hammer'. It was
the same in the case of R. Johanan (ben Nappacha)
(died c. A.D. 290), the Palestinian Amora ('interpreter'),
in whose academy the Jerusalem Talmud originated.
When he was dying he begged to be buried neither in
white[5] nor in black garments, but in garments dyed a
shimmering colour, so as to be neither white nor black;
then if he was given his place amongst the righteous he
would not have to be ashamed, and if he was placed

[1] Hence too the warning of Hillel: Do not rely on yourself even
up to the day of your death (Ab. 2.4).

[2] This is a characteristic of the whole of rabbinic Judaism (cf.
the passages in Str-B. III, pp. 218 ff.).

[3] A. Schlatter, *Jochanan ben Zakkai, der Zeitgenosse der Apostel*
(1899).

[4] The plural covers a guarded way of speaking about God, as
does also e.g. the δώσουσιν of Luke vi.38 (cf. Dalman, *Worte Jesu* I,
p. 183 f.).

[5] The rabbis, like the NT, considered the garments of the
righteous to be white.

amongst the sinners (*r^esha̅'im*) he would not be shamed[1] (J. Kil. 32b, 8 ff.).[2] In both cases the lack of assurance remains final. 'A confidence based on works does not ensure certainty and fear gains the victory over faith.'[3] It makes no real difference to this state of affairs that we also possess accounts of rabbis who when dying felt confident about their future.[4] The basic mood of the rabbinate when considering the judgement is pessimistic,[5] and this mood finds its classic expression in the constantly continuing casuistical discussions. There is perhaps no more striking illustration than the story that the schools of Hillel and Shammai had disputed for more than two years whether it would be better for man not to have been created, or whether it was good for him to have been created; and that they had agreed upon the conclusion that it would be better for him not to have been created (B. Erub. 13b Bar.). Indeed no other attitude is possible 'under the law'.

The fact that within the sphere of nomism no universal hope exists[6] has been expressed by no one more

---

[1] The statement presupposes the view that man 'comes back' as he 'goes'; this view had been generally accepted.

[2] cf. also Gn. r. 96.5 on xlvii.29; and 100.1 on xlix.33.

[3] A. Schlatter, *op. cit.*, p. 73 on the death of Johanan ben Zakkai.

[4] cf. the two accounts in Gn. r. 100.1 on xlix.33 and parallels.

[5] In addition cf. the fact that it was Akiba who frequently quoted Ecclesiastes with approval: see *Jew. Enc.* I, p. 305.

[6] In connexion with this statement it is interesting to note that Akiba used the description of God as *miqwēh yisrā'ēl (hope of Israel)* in Jer. xvii.13 in the sense of an *immersion-pool*: Yoma 8.9: 'And it is said: *miqweh yisrā'ēl* is Yahweh. What is meant by the *miqweh*? It cleanses the unclean. Thus does the Holy One, praised be He, also cleanse Israel.' At the same time in the context in question the literal meaning of this formula would have been most suitable. [Note: *miqwāh* occurs in Isa. xxii.11 in the sense of *reservoir*, from a root meaning 'to collect'.]

clearly than by the Johannine Jesus (John v.45): ἔστιν
ὁ κατηγορῶν ὑμῶν Μωϋσῆς, εἰς ὃν ὑμεῖς ἠλπίκατε. Here the
absurdity of hope on the basis of the religion of the law
is stated with the utmost trenchancy: he who depends
on man for his eternal future will always remain the
defendant in the sight of God; and if anyone wants to
procure his salvation himself by means of the law, then
no one less than Moses himself will accuse him, because
he has not understood that in Moses' view God alone
leads man to his goal and that God alone gives him the
credit which preserves him from destruction (cf. John
v.44).

(b) The rabbinate with full awareness of its position
took various paths in order to overcome its lack of
assurance of salvation. Thus Akiba advocated the
thesis that man becomes sure of God's favour in prayer.[1]
Akin to this[2] is the effort to draw conclusions about his
eternal fate from the manner of a man's dying.[3] The
most vigorous attempt at abolishing the agonising uncertainty is however the so-called 'theology of suffering'.[4] This[5] undertakes to interpret the suffering which
befalls the godly; and it does so in fact particularly by
explaining it as the discipline which gives him the

[1] T. Ber. 3.3.
[2] Akiba's thesis is closely related to that of the famous man of
prayer, Choni, who recognised that his prayer was acceptable
when it was 'fluent', i.e. when he could pray without faltering
(B. Ber. 34b Bar.).
[3] cf. the catalogue in B. Ket. 103b, and also the passages in
Wichmann, p. 3, n. 4.
[4] The name goes back to the phrase 'Theology of suffering'
('Theologie des Leidens'), coined by P. Volz in *Jüdische Eschatologie
von Daniel bis Akiba* (1903), p. 155.
[5] Evidence for this exists also outside the rabbinate, but here it
was most widespread (Wichmann, p. 51).

possibility already in this life of paying the penalty for his guilt for which he would otherwise have had to atone completely after his death.[1] Here the wish predominates to reduce the unknown number of lapses and thus to give an increasing preponderance to a man's merits, with the result that the just God will not be able to help acquitting him and admitting him into the Garden of Eden, this being of course only what God wishes to do.[2] It is significant that this doctrine was most lastingly defined and developed by Akiba and his school.[3] According to the tradition[4] he smiled as he stood at the death-bed of his teacher, Eliezer ben Hyrcanus, writhing in pain, and explained his smile by saying that he was glad of these pains, because he saw in them a guarantee that God was mercifully disposed towards his teacher. Perhaps this lay also at the root of his own attitude during his martyrdom, and of that particular feature of it which made it appear as the expression of self-justification before God (cf. p. 20). It must be admitted that this attempt of the rabbinate at overcoming their hopelessness also faded into the background again comparatively quickly. Its latest advocate is as early as Rabba ben Joseph ben Chama, a

---

[1] This must not be confused with the idea of a retribution already in this life; this idea is never found within the framework of the 'theology of suffering' (Wichmann, p. 11).

[2] This whole way of looking at the matter is based on the conviction of God's absolute justice (cf. above, pp. 22 f.). God as the Just One gives the godly man by his suffering the opportunity to atone for unknown trespasses in order not to be obliged to reject him. Since God alone has the power to decide who is to participate in atoning suffering, this doctrine actually acquires a predestin arian character.

[3] Wichmann, pp. 56 ff.

[4] B. Sanh. 101a; cf. on this Wichmann, pp. 62f.

Babylonian Amora, at the beginning of the fourth century.[1] The theory failed in the long run because, although it could explain the suffering of the godly, it could not give to their good fortune also a meaning based on God.[2] Thus the theory broke down as a result of its own anthropocentrism. Hence we can recognise once again the point at which the hopelessness of the rabbinate is to be found, namely that it never got away from itself. For hope is possible only when a man has learned that he can contribute nothing to his own salvation, but that God does everything and that it is God's purpose to lead man to this salvation not by way of his achievement, but by granting it to him *sola gratia.*

[1] Wichmann, p. 78.
[2] Wichmann, pp. 77 f.

IV. THE HOPE OF HELLENISTIC JUDAISM

1. *General usage*

Hellenistic Judaism too was of course aware that hope belongs to life (Ecclus. xiv.2) and is destroyed only by death (Ps. Sol. xvii.2). The sick man hopes for recovery (II Macc. ix.22). One man inspires hopes in another (Ecclus. xiii.6). Those who are parted hope (or hope no longer) to see each other again (Tob. x.7).[1] It is true that *A man of no understanding has vain and false hopes* (Ecclus. xxxiv.1 : a free rendering of the Hebrew). The hope of the ungodly is vain (Wisd. iii.1; cf. v.14, xvi.29) or uncertain (II Macc. vii.34); if they die they have no ἐλπίς (Wisd. iii.18). The ἐλπίδες of idol-worshippers are set on dead things (Wisd. xiii.10; cf. xv.6, 10) and it is useless to place one's hope on military power (Judith ix.7). But the ἐλπίς of the godly is fixed on God, their saviour.[2] They have good hopes (Letter of Aristeas 261), so they have nothing to fear (Ecclus. xxxiv.16; I Macc. ii.61 f.); for their hope is united with the fear of God (Ecclus. xxxiv.14 f.; Ps. Sol. vi.8; similarly also of the Messiah in Ps. Sol. xvii.44). God is indeed the *hope of all who continue in his ways* (Test. Jud. xxvi.1). 'Ελπίς possesses the quality of confidence (Ecclus. xlix.10; Judith xiii.19; II Macc. xv.7: *trusting with all hope*). The hope of the mighty rests in God (Ps. Sol. xvii.38), but He is above all the *hope of the needy and the poor* (Ps. Sol. v.13, xv.2, xviii.3 *et passim*). Whilst in

---

[1] A variant reading is πιστεύειν. Cf. *Faith* in this series.

[2] Ecclus. xxxiv.13 f.; Ps. Sol. xvii.3; cf. v.16, viii.37, ix.19, xv.1; Susanna 60; Test. Asher vii.7 (variant reading).

these cases the object of hope is usually God's protection and help in general,[1] it can naturally also be help
in a particular situation of need (II Macc. xv.7; Judith
viii.20; Letter of Aristeas 18: μεγάλη ἐλπίς; Jos. Ant.
12.300: *their hopes of victory in God*).[2] Hope can spring
up in the hour of death (II Macc. ix.20). Such hope is
denied to the ungodly (Wisd. iii.18; cf. xv.10), but the
hope of the godly is *full of immortality* (Wisd. iii.4); it is
directed towards the resurrection (II Macc. vii.11, 14,
20), it is the *hope of salvation from God* (IV Macc. xi.7).
Beside this there is the lively eschatological hope of the
restoration of Israel (II Macc. ii.18; Test. Benjamin
x.11), or of the time of salvation; the evidence for this
is supplied by the rabbinic, and especially by the
apocalyptic literature.[3]

2. *Philo*

In Philo Greek psychology makes itself felt, in so far
as for him ἐλπίς is essentially *expectation* (*Leg. All.* II.43)[4];
nevertheless he also uses the word ἐλπίς in accordance

[1] Here too it can be said that God is the ἐλπίς (cf. p. 11, n. 4);
cf. the Greek translation of Ps. xiv.6, xxii.9; in addition Ecclus.
xxxiv.16; Ps. Sol. v.13, xv.2.

[2] Josephus generally observes the Greek linguistic usage. Thus
for him ἐλπίς also means the expectation of something evil: *Ant.*
2.211, 6.215, 11.247. It is the expectation of something desirable
in *Ant.* 17.1; in *Bell.* 6.264, 383. Thus the frequent Greek phrase
παρ' ἐλπίδα(ς) in *Ant.* 7.179, 198 *et passim* (also κατ' ἐλπίδα in *Ant.*
16.322). 'Ελπὶς σωτηρίας as in Greek in *Ant.* 16.389; *Bell.* 7.165,
331; ἐλπὶς βεβαία (sure) in *Bell.* 7.413; *Ant.* 8.280. Whilst Jos. *Ant.*
8.282, 12.300 uses the OT phrase 'to have hopes in God' in *Bell.*
2.391, 6.99 he says: '(God) *whom you looked to as ally*'.

[3] Bousset-Gressmann, pp. 202 ff.; Pott, *op. cit.*, pp. 10 ff. According to Ethiopic Enoch xl.9 there is an angel *who is set over the
penitence and hope of those who inherit eternal life.*

[4] 'Ελπίζειν = to await in *Leg. All.* III.87; *Cher.* 75; *Det. Pot. Ins.*
160; *Fug.* 164 *et passim.*

with later Greek usage ordinarily for the expectation of good (*Abr.* 14). Thus he considers ἐλπίς and χαρά (*joy*) to be similar (*Det. Pot. Ins.* 140) and he is particularly fond of describing ἐλπίς (as contrasted with φόβος (*fear*) in *Abr.* 14; *Mut. Nom.* 163) as the pleasure of anticipation.[1] As in Greek ἐλπίς corresponds in his view to μνήμη (*memory*); it is also in accordance with Greek[2] thought to consider ἐλπίς as a comfort in trouble (*Jos.* 20.144); for in all cases hope is here directed to a picture of the future planned by men: without such a hope life is not worth living (*Praem. Poen.* 72).

However, where Philo deals with hope particularly, he is not concerned with ideas of the future which display human and earthly desires; the object of ἐλπίς is rather that man should attain perfection (*Rer. Div. Her.* 311); and in this sense ἐλπίς is one of the qualities of the one who is truly a man, of the rational nature (*Det. Pot. Ins.* 138 f.). He who does not 'hope in God' is not a proper man; Philo exemplifies this several times by Enoch ('Ενώς = ἄνθρωπος), who according to Gen. iv.26 was the first to hope in God.[3] Enoch is the *one who always desired the excellent but has not yet been able to attain to it* (*Abr.* 47). 'Ελπίς should be directed towards God, whilst the body is concerned with desire (*Poster. C.* 26). Yet Philo can also speak more generally in the OT sense of the hope which addresses itself to God as saviour (*Leg. Gai.* 196), who bestows gifts contrary to

---

[1] *Leg. All.* III.86 f.; *Mut. Nom.* 161-5; *Exsecr.* 180. Thus he also not infrequently uses εὔελπις and εὐελπιστία, see Leisegang, *Index* (1926).

[2] *Leg. All.* II.42 f. where it is joined by αἴσθησις (*perception*) as a third term (cf. p. 1); in *Migr. Abr.* 154 the *expectation of things to come* appears as a third term.

[3] *Det. Pot. Ins.* 138 f.; *Abr.* 7-14; *Praem. Poen.* 11-14.

and beyond what is hoped for,[1] to God's gracious nature
(*Spec. Leg.* I.310, II.196) or to the gentleness of His
nature (*Fug.* 99), the hope in particular which expects
forgiveness (*Fug.* 99; *Spec. Leg.* II.196). This hope is
intimately connected with πίστις (*Leg. All.* III.164).
The ἐλπίδες of the wicked are certainly not fulfilled
(*Exsecr.* 142, 149; cf. *Praem. Poen.* 12[2]). Eschatological
hopes play no part in Philo, but Moses has *the hope of
coming immortality* (*Virt.* 67).

---

[1] *Leg. All.* III.85; *Sacr. A.C.* 78; *Somn.* I.71; *Decal.* 16; *Spec. Leg.*
II.219; cf. also H. Windisch, *Die Frömmigkeit Philos* (1909), pp.
53 ff.)

[2] Unfulfilled hopes are mentioned elsewhere too, e.g. *Epigr.
Graec.* 497.5: the unfulfilled hopes of parents whose daughter has
died.

V. THE EARLY CHRISTIAN CONCEPT OF HOPE

1. *General usage*

The concept of hope in the NT is determined in its essentials by that of the OT.[1] Only when hope in the profane sense is in question does the element of expectation, a characteristic of the Greek ἐλπίζειν, usually predominate. Yet the word ἐλπίζειν is always used only when something acceptable is expected and the differentiation between ἀγαθή and πονηρὰ ἐλπίς is lacking.

Thus ἐλπίζειν (ἐλπίς) in the profane sense means 'to expect' with a hint of 'to reckon on' in Luke vi.34; I Cor. ix.10; II Cor. viii.5; I Tim. iii.14; Acts xvi.19; Herm. v. III.11.3. There is no doubt a stronger emphasis on 'hoping' in Luke xxiii.8; Acts xxiv.26, xxvii.20; this is more evident still in Luke xxiv.21; Rom. xv.24; I Cor. xvi.7; Phil. ii.19, 23; Philemon 22; II John 12; III John 14; Ign. Eph. i.2, x.1; Rom. i.1; Barn. xvii.1. But when such expectation refers to the behaviour of people, the confidence, characteristic of the OT concept, comes to the fore: II Cor. i.13, v.11, xiii.6 and especially II Cor. i.7, x.15, as the interchange with the

[1] For grammatical questions cf. the grammars. 'Ελπίζειν is employed as in the LXX with its object denoted by ἐπί with the dative or accusative or by ἐν or εἰς (cf. p. 11, n. 3). The dative alone is used once: Matt. xii.21. 'Ελπίς can denote not only the attitude of hopefulness, but also rhetorically the thing hoped for (Rom. viii.24; Col. i.5; Titus ii.13; Heb. vi.18; in the LXX II Macc. vii.14); this is also a common Greek usage (e.g. Aesch. *Choeph.* 778; cf. p. 6, n. 5, and for the alternation of ἐλπίς and ἔλπισμα cf. Plut. *Suav. Viv. Epic.* 6 (II.1090 d), cf. p. 4, n. 3. The concept of hope is not modified by this usage.

33

idea of πεποίθησις shows; for this word in i.15 refers back
to ἐλπίζειν (verse 13) and takes the place of ἐλπίς in
viii.22, x.2 (cf. e.g. i.7, x.15). In I Cor. xiii.7 hope, like
love, clearly has a person as its object, although this
attitude is based for Paul too on the corresponding
attitude towards God, as the natural transition from
the one to the other indicates. And the insertion of
πάντα ἐλπίζει, fitted in between πάντα πιστεύει and πάντα
ὑπομένει, demonstrates that the three verbs describe an
attitude which is all of one piece.

2. The nature of hope

If hope is fixed on God, it comprises just these three
elements combined in one: expectation of what is to
come, confidence and patience in waiting; and first one
and then another can be emphasised or explicitly
brought into relief. The definition of πίστις in Heb. xi.1
as ἐλπιζομένων ὑπόστασις corresponds fully to the OT
idea that πιστεύειν and ἐλπίζειν belong together (Ps.
lxxviii.22) and the usage of the LXX which renders
tiqwāh (Ezek. xix.5; Ruth i.12) and tōḥelet (Ps. xxxviii.7
[EVV 8]) with ὑπόστασις[1] beside ἐλπίς (p. 9). It is
emphasised that the confidence placed in the future
bestowed by God can be trusted,[2] and the added phrase
ἔλεγχος[3] πραγμάτων οὐ βλεπομένων lays still further stress
on the paradoxical nature of this hopeful confidence,
in so far as it simply cannot reckon on what is under

[1] Ὑποστῆναι appears for yḥl (p. 9) in Micah v.7 (Heb. 6); so
too for ḥsh (p. 9) in Judges ix.15.
[2] cf. in the following verses particularly, verse 10: ἧς τεχνίτης ...
θεός; verse 11: ἐπεὶ πιστὸν ἡγήσατο τὸν ἐπαγγειλάμενον; verse 19:
λογισάμενος ὅτι...; verse 23: οὐκ ἐφοβήθησαν...; verse 27:
μὴ φοβηθεὶς κτλ.
[3] This word is used in the LXX mainly for tokaḥat (proof).

man's control.¹ It is just this element in ἐλπίς which Paul too brings out in his 'definition' in Rom. viii.24 f.: ἐλπὶς δὲ βλεπομένη οὐκ ἔστιν ἐλπίς· ὃ γὰρ βλέπει τις, τί καὶ ἐλπίζει; In this question there is first of all an argument of formal logic (suitable to the context), which states that hope, as an attitude directed to the future, can only after all be spoken of when its object is not actually present. Yet in Paul's view its positive meaning lies in the fact that ἐλπίς cannot be directed to βλεπόμενα because these are πρόσκαιρα (II Cor. iv.18); for whatever is seen belongs surely to the sphere of flesh (σάρξ²), on which no hope can be based. But Paul goes on to lay stress on the element of patient waiting which also belongs to ἐλπίς (on I Cor. xiii.7 cf. p. 34) when he continues: εἰ δὲ ὃ οὐ βλέπομεν ἐλπίζομεν, δι' ὑπομονῆς ἀπεκδεχόμεθα. This quality in ἐλπίς permits him to employ also the paradox in Rom. iv.18: ὃς παρ' ἐλπίδα ἐπ' ἐλπίδι ἐπίστευσεν; when the limit of reckoning with what is under our own control had been reached, then confidence in God's future stepped in. The element of firm confidence also determines the meaning of ἐλπίζειν in I Cor. xv.19; II Cor. i.10, iii.12; Phil. i.20; Heb. iii.6; I Peter i.21: ὥστε τὴν πίστιν ὑμῶν καὶ ἐλπίδα εἶναι εἰς θεόν,³ whilst the idea of patient waiting receives the

¹ cf. again in the following verses, verse 7: περὶ τῶν μηδέπω βλεπομένων; verse 8: μὴ ἐπιστάμενος ...; verse 19: παραβολῇ ἐκομίσατο; verse 25: μᾶλλον ... ἢ πρόσκαιρον ἔχειν ... ἀπόλαυσιν; verse 27: τὸν ... ἀόρατον ὡς ὁρῶν ἐκαρτέρησεν.

² cf. TWNT VII. Cf. also J. A. T. Robinson, The Body (1952).

³ It is possible in this passage to take τὴν πίστιν ὑμῶν and (τὴν) ἐλπίδα as the co-ordinated subject of εἶναι. In that case πίστις and ἐλπίς together describe that OT concept of confident hope. Alternatively ἐλπίδα can be considered to be the predicate: so that your faith is at the same time hope in God. This affirms that faith includes confident waiting on God's future.

chief emphasis in Rom. v.4 f., xv.4; I Thess. i.3 (τῆς ὑπομονῆς τῆς ἐλπίδος), v.8 (ἐλπίδα σωτηρίας, cf. Ps. lxxviii.22); Heb. vi.11, x.23. But of course we must not think that either element is ever eliminated.[1]

Whilst in this respect the structure of the ἐλπίς concept does not differ from that of the OT, there is a difference from the OT in the circumstances of the man who hopes, as demonstrated particularly in II Cor. iii.1-18. The πεποίθησις in verse 4 and the ἐλπίς in verse 12 of which Paul boasts no doubt include also his hopeful confidence in the Corinthians (i.13, 15), but they are in a much more fundamental sense the apostolic reliance and certainty which he has as διάκονος of the καινὴ διαθήκη. They have the same meaning as the ἐλευθερία[2] (verse 17) which is freedom from the law, and from death, so that παρρησία (verse 12, vii.4) and καύχησις (i.12, vii.4, x.8 ff., xi.16 ff.) are based on it.[3] Thus Christian ἐλπίς rests on God's act of salvation effected in Christ, and since this is an eschatological act, ἐλπίς itself appears as an eschatological blessing, i.e. now is the time in which one may have confident trust.[4] The waiting, which is part of ἐλπίς, is therefore

---

[1] Ἐλπίζειν (ἐλπίς) meaning 'trust' occurs also in I Clem. xi.1, xii.7 (combined with πιστεύειν); II Clem. xvii.7; Barn. vi.3; Herm. m. XII.5.2, 6.4; Just. Dial. 35.2. The contrast in John v.45: Μωϋσῆς, εἰς ὃν ὑμεῖς ἠλπίκατε: on whom you base your security (cf. pp. 25 f.); cf. Barn. xvi.1 f.

[2] cf. TWNT II, pp. 492 ff.

[3] cf. with this particularly II Cor. xi.17: ἐν ταύτῃ τῇ ὑποστάσει τῆς καυχήσεως (cf. pp. 8f.) and for the concept of καύχησις (TWNT III pp. 646 ff.) cf. Rom. v.2: καυχώμεθα ἐπ' ἐλπίδα τῆς δόξης τοῦ θεοῦ and Heb. iii.6: τὸ καύχημα τῆς ἐλπίδος. In the LXX ἐλπίς and ὑπόστασις as well as καύχησις are used for tōḥelet (Prov. xi.7), cf. p. 9.

[4] cf. p. 11, n. 3. When Paul quotes Isa. xi.10 in Rom. xv.12 it indicates that in his view that promise is now fulfilled.

itself achieved by the spirit, the gift of the last days[1] and is based on πίστις in the act of salvation (Gal. v.5), just as being in ἐλπίς in Rom. viii.24 f. is then immediately described in verses 26 f. as being assisted by the πνεῦμα. Thus ἐλπίς together with πίστις makes up the Christian being. Hence the expression of blessing in Rom. xv.13; hence the characteristic quality of the Christians is that they are τῇ ἐλπίδι χαίροντες in Rom. xii.12, and hence that of the pagans is μὴ ἔχοντες ἐλπίδα in I Thess. iv.13,[2] which of course does not mean that they do not make for themselves any pictures of a future after death, but that they can have no well-founded confidence in the future. In so far as πίστις is active in ἀγάπη[3] (Gal. v.6), πίστις, ἀγάπη and ἐλπίς make up the Christian being, as Paul describes it in I Thess. i.3, and as he sets out its qualities in I Cor. xiii.13, no doubt as an antithesis to a Gnostic formula.[4] The basic OT concept of hope also enables us to understand why Paul can say that ἐλπίς too remains, even though one day βλέπειν will be achieved (I Cor. xiii.12); for ἐλπίς is not directed towards realising a picture of the future as projected by man, but is the trust in God which turns away from itself and the world, which waits patiently for God's gift, and which, when He has given it, does not consider it to be a possession at one's own disposal, but is confidently assured that God also will maintain what He has bestowed. Christian being—in accordance with its understanding of God—can never be conceived as perfect apart from ἐλπίς. Before it is achieved, emphasis

---

[1] So also Barn. xi.11.

[2] So also in Eph. ii.12 (with the characteristic addition that the pagans are ἄθεοι); II Clem. i.7.

[3] cf. *Love* in this series, esp. p. 59.   [4] cf. p. 6, n. 3.

may be placed on tarrying and patient waiting on the
future: Rom. v.2, 4 f., viii.20, 24 f.; I Cor. xv.19; Gal.
v.5; I Thess. ii.19, which indeed would not be the case,
if in the phrase τῇ γὰρ ἐλπίδι ἐσώθημεν (Rom. viii.24)
the word ἐσώθημεν was not stressed and if παρρησία and
καύχησις did not spring from it.

3. *The eschatological element*

Apart from Paul, in the NT the concept of ἐλπίς has
little place in the Johannine writings (on John v.45
cf. p. 36, n. 1). It appears in them as a hope fixed on
future fulfilment only in I John iii.3. But what ἐλπίζειν
denotes can in fact be subsumed in the πίστις concept,
and so it is in John.[1] That in Revelation ἐλπίς is lacking
altogether can astonish only those who overlook the
fact that the idea of hope is included here in the ὑπομονή
concept.

Elsewhere, especially where Jewish influence is strong,
the element of waiting for the eschatological future is
very pronounced: Col. i.5; I Tim. iv.10; Titus ii.13, iii.7;
I Peter i.3, 13; Heb. vi.18 f., vii.19[2]; in Acts it has one
object only, namely the resurrection from the dead:
xxiii.6, xxiv.15, xxvi.6 f., xxviii.20; just as, in Acts ii.26,
Ps. xvi.9 (EVV 10) is explained as referring to the resurrection of Christ.[3] The paradox that Christian ἐλπίς
is itself already an eschatological blessing, because in
it the OT hope is known to be fulfilled by the sending
of Jesus, is found most clearly in Matt. xii.21, which
applies Isa. xlii.4 to Jesus (cf. Rom. xv.12) and in

---

[1] See *Faith* in this series, esp. pp. 97 ff.
[2] With the same meaning in Barn. viii.5; Just. *Dial.* 44.4;
Athenag. 33.1; Sib. Or. ii.53.
[3] Ἐλπίς in I Clem. xxvii.1 also has the resurrection in view.

I Peter i.3: (ὁ θεός) ὁ ἀναγεννήσας ἡμᾶς εἰς ἐλπίδα ζῶσαν δι' ἀναστάσεως Ἰησοῦ Χριστοῦ ἐκ νεκρῶν.¹ In a somewhat more conventional manner it is used also in those cases in which Christ himself is designated as our ἐλπίς,² in which the ἐλπίς bestowed on us is mentioned³ and in which ἐλπίς, associated with other concepts⁴ or alone⁵ appears as the distinctive mark of Christianity. Such phrases are sometimes almost like formulae; this is evident particularly in Barn. i.4, 6, where πίστις is no longer the basis of ἐλπίς, as with Paul, but on the contrary πίστις is resting on ἐλπίς.

The fact that—apart from Revelation—no detailed pictures of the future are sketched shows that the quality of trusting in God's action is preserved as an inherent element of hopeful waiting, and this is occasionally brought out strongly by the way it is formulated.⁶ Similarly the quality of patient waiting is sometimes

---

¹ Ign. Mg. ix.1; Barn. xvi.8.
² Col. i.27; I Tim. i.1; Ign. Eph. xxi.2; Mg. xi.1; Tr. Introduction ii.2; Phld. xi.2; cf. p. 11, n. 4, p. 30, n. 1. Hope in Jesus (ἐπὶ or εἰς) in Barn. vi.3, xi.11; Just. Dial. 16.4, 47.2 et passim; in his cross: Barn. xi.8; cf. Just. Dial. 96.1, 110.3; in his name (ὄνομα) in Barn. xvi.8 (I Clem. lix.3: in the name of God: a Jewish feature). ³ II Thess. ii.16; cf. I Clem. lvii.2.
⁴ Col. i.4 f. (ἀκούσαντες τὴν πίστιν ὑμῶν . . . καὶ τὴν ἀγάπην ἣν ἔχετε . . . διὰ τὴν ἐλπίδα). Titus i.1 f. (ἀπόστολος . . . κατὰ πίστιν ἐκλεκτῶν θεοῦ καὶ ἐπίγνωσιν ἀληθείας τῆς κατ' εὐσέβειαν ἐπ' ἐλπίδι ζωῆς αἰωνίου). Heb. x.22-24; Ign. Mg. vii.1; Phld. xi.2; I Clem. lviii.2 (the wording of an oath); Barn. iv.8, xi.8; Just. Dial. 110.3; especially the variations on the triad of 1 Cor. xiii.13; Barn. i.4, i.6; Pol. iii.2 f.
⁵ Col. i.23; Eph. i.18, iv.4; especially I Peter iii.15 (. . . λόγον περὶ τῆς ἐν ὑμῖν ἐλπίδος); I Clem. li.1; Ign. Eph. i.2; Phld. v.2. For the concept: κοινὴ ἐλπίς see Thuc. II.43.6; Lys. 2.9.
⁶ I Peter i.3; Titus i.2, ii.13 f., iii.5-7. The fact that ἐλπίς and πίστις belong together appears from the way they are mentioned in Barn. iv.8.

emphasised.[1] The fact that ἐλπίς does not stand by itself in the Christian life, but develops into a fresh attitude to the world, is not only expressed in those stereotyped descriptions of Christian behaviour, but is now and then explicitly stressed.[2]

[1] Col. i.23; Heb. vi.18 f., x.23. Ign. Phld. v.2; Pol. viii.1; II Clem. xi.5.

[2] I John iii.3 (πᾶς ὁ ἔχων τὴν ἐλπίδα ταύτην ἐπ' αὐτῷ ἁγνίζει ἑαυτόν...); Eph. iv.1-4; I Tim. v.5 (a contrast in vi.17); Titus ii.11-14; I Peter i.13; Ign. Mg. ix.1; Barn. xi.11; Athenag. 33.1. Herm. says repeatedly that sin causes hope to be lost: v. I.1.9, m. V.1.7, s. VIII.9.4, IX.14.3, IX.26.2. But for Herm. there is a fresh hope, the hope of penitence: s. VI.2.4, VIII.6.5, VIII.7.2, VIII.10.2.

APPENDIX

(a) Ἀπελπίζω is first found in the later Greek literature, in which it is used beside the verbs ἀπογινώσκειν and ἀπονοεῖσθαι, which were common earlier, with the same meaning.[1] The meaning is: *not to believe*, or *hope*, that something will happen; thus generally that of the Latin *desperare* (as well apparently as *desperare facio*)[2]; it takes the accusative and is also used in the passive. Amongst its many possible applications[3] that to illness or, alternatively, to recovery is especially frequent; a sick man who is 'given up' is an ἀπελπισθείς or ἀπηλπισμένος.[4]

In the Septuagint ἀπελπίζειν occurs with the general meaning of *giving up hope* in Ecclus. xxii.21, xxvii.21 (both times referring to a friendship in danger) and in II Macc. ix.18 with reference to illness. It is noteworthy that in Isa. xxix.19 *the poor among men* is rendered by ἀπηλπισμένοι τῶν ἀνθρώπων, and its use in Judith ix.11, where God is invoked, agrees with this: *thou art a God of the afflicted, thou art a helper of the oppressed, an*

---

[1] Attested first in Hyperides 5.35 (p. 88 Jensen). Cf. L. Götzeler, *De Polybi Elocutione* (Diss. Erlangen, 1887), p. 23; P. Linde, *Breslauer philol. Abhandlungen* IX.3 (1906), pp. 31 f.

[2] So evidently in *Anth. Pal.* XI.114.6 and certainly in the patristic literature, see Thes. Steph., s.v.

[3] cf. Polyb. 23.13.2; Andronicus, *De Passionibus*, p. 14, 14 (Kreuttner); Nero in Ditt Syll (ed. 3, p. 814, 10 f.); cf. p. 7.

[4] E.g. Ditt Syll ed. 3, p. 1173, 7.11: further material in O. Weinreich, *Antike Heilungswunder* (1909), pp. 195 f.; K. Kerényi, *Die Griech.-oriental. Romanliteratur* (1927) p. 27, n. 11. Ἀπογινώσκειν is also used in the same sense. This word is not found in the NT, but it is in the LXX and in Herm. (see Pr-Bauer).

41

upholder of the weak, a protector of the forlorn, a saviour of the despairing (ἀπηλπισμένων).[1]

In the NT ἀπηλπικότες appears in Eph. iv.19 as a variant reading (D 257 Lat syr^p), in place of ἀπηλγηκότες, (to *become callous*), as a distinctive mark of pagans; it is used absolutely, as in Isa. xxix.19 and in Judith ix.11. God is also described in I Clem. lix.3 as *saviour of τῶν ἀπηλπισμένων*, as he is in Judith ix.11. Figuratively in Herm. v. III.12.2 an old man who has lost all hope is described as ἀφηλπικὼς ἑαυτόν. In the Apologists the word does not occur.

Its use in Luke vi.35 is unique: δανίζετε μηδὲν ἀπελπίζοντες. For according to verse 34 (ἐὰν δανίσητε παρ᾽ ὧν ἐλπίζετε λαβεῖν) it can only be understood as *lend without expecting to be repaid* (or if interest were in mind *without expecting any return*).[2]

Thus ἀπελπίζειν would be used in accordance with the analogy of ἀπαιτεῖν and similar words (a usage authenticated only from Chrysostom onwards)[3] or it is an example of abbreviation (ἀπελπίζω = ἀπολαμβάνειν ἐλπίζω) and that is how the Vulgate translates it: *nihil inde sperantes*. The usual meaning of ἀπελπίζειν could only lead to the translation *where you despair of nothing* (Old Latin: *nihil desperantes*) which could probably only mean:

---

[1] In Josephus ἀπελπίζειν is often found with the usual meaning of 'giving up hope', see Schlatter, *Lukas*, p. 249 (on Luke vi.35). Philo, according to Leisegang's *Index*, does not use ἀπελπίζειν; he uses ἀπογινώσκειν often with τὰς ἐλπίδας as its object (see Leisegang). This occurs in the LXX only in Deut. xxxiii.9 (for *ignored*); Judith ix.11 (cf. above); II Macc. ix.22.

[2] In that case there would be a parallel to this saying in a rabbinic precept handed down several times: 'He . . . who lends without interest is considered (by God) to have kept all the commandments' (Str-B. II, p. 159).

[3] See Zahn, *Lukas* (1913), *ad loc.*

where you hope for a heavenly compensation.[1] But this suits the context no better than the sense which, following the reading μηδένα ἀπελπίζοντες (LA X, syrᵖ etc.) would yield the meaning: *where you despair of no one, do not give up hope for anyone* (or if ἀπελπίζειν is taken transitively, *where you bring none to despair*). Since the first meaning is linguistically satisfactory, the proposed conjecture ἀνελπίζοντες, which would give the same meaning, is unnecessary.

(*b*) Προσελπίζω, *to hope for beforehand*, seems to be attested only by Posidippus (third century B.C.) in Athen. IX.20 (377c) apart from Christian literature.

According to Eph. i.12 'we' are chosen by the will of God: εἰς τὸ εἶναι ἡμᾶς εἰς ἔπαινον δόξης αὐτοῦ, τοὺς προηλπικότας ἐν τῷ Χριστῷ.[2] If the author includes himself with the Jewish Christians as belonging to a special group of believers, then he is using the προ- to mean either *earlier than the Gentiles* or *already before Christ was sent*, which would fit in well with the thought that Christ is the fulfilment of the OT hope (cf. pp. 36 f.). If on the other hand 'we' is understood to mean all Christians, then προ- is used from the standpoint of the present with the eschatological fulfilment in view. But this is probably less likely. The word does not occur in the Apostolic Fathers nor in the Apologists.

---

[1] See Klostermann, *Lukas* (²1929), *ad loc.*
[2] For the construction with ἐν, cf. p. 33, n. 1.

INDEX OF REFERENCES

45

NEW TESTAMENT

APOCRYPHA AND PSEUDEPIGRAPHA

GENERAL INDEX

II

LIFE

AND

DEATH

BY

RUDOLF BULTMANN

WITH CONTRIBUTIONS BY

G. VON RAD and G. BERTRAM

Translated from the German by
P.H. Ballard *and* D. Turner *and* L.A. Garrard (CHAPTER II)
Edited by P.R. Ackroyd

EDITOR'S PREFACE

THIS book contains a translation of the main part of two articles in the *Theologisches Wörterbuch zum Neuen Testament* (TWNT), begun by G. Kittel and now edited by G. Friedrich. The two articles are Ζωή in Vol. II, pp. 833-877, and Θάνατος in Vol. III, pp. 7-25. The major part of the two articles was written by R. Bultmann, but what appears here as Chapter I, 1-3 is by G. von Rad, and what appears as Chapter III, 1 is by G. Bertram.

In their original form, the two articles were seen to cover a good deal of common ground, and for this reason the Old Testament and some other material was gathered entirely in the first, covering both Life and Death. It seemed therefore convenient to combine the articles into one volume in translation, and to arrange the material in a slightly different order, following a pattern which has been used more than once in this series. Chapter I, the Old Testament material, appears complete; Chapter II contains a very much shortened version of the two sections on Greek usage; Chapter III is taken almost entirely from the article on Life, but its last section, on Philo, covers some material from the article on Death. Chapters IV and V are complete, though some shortening has been made in the Additional Notes appended to them. It is hoped that this outline will enable any reader who wishes to do so to find the relevant places in the German text.

The bibliographical material and the footnotes have been very slightly supplemented, in particular with some reference to more recent works in which further literature is cited. It is evident that further reference needs to be made both to the Qumran literature and also

to the Gnostic literature now becoming accessible with
its modifying of our understanding of the nature of that
kind of thought. What is said in these chapters about
the nature of life and in particular about the relationship between Christian and Gnostic interpretations of
its meaning, is clearly of relevance to the larger discussion
of what is meant in a Christian theological context by
the term 'life'.

All Hebrew words have been transliterated and,
where necessary, translated. Greek words are not transliterated. Where quotations are given from elsewhere
than the New Testament (or Septuagint), a translation
has sometimes been given, but the amount of such
quotation in this particular volume has suggested the
propriety of referring the reader to translations of the
texts where he finds he needs such assistance. Some
cross-reference has been made to other volumes in this
series, and to other articles in TWNT; many of the
fundamental terms may be studied further in Bible
word books, dictionaries, and Old and New Testament
theologies.

P.R.A.

CONTENTS

BIBLIOGRAPHY

CHAPTER I

W. W. COUNT BAUDISSIN: 'Alttestamentliches hajjim "Leben" in der Bedeutung von Glück' in *Festschrift E. Sachau* (1915), pp. 143-161.

A. BERTHOLET: *Die israelitischen Vorstellungen vom Zustand nach dem Tode* (²1914).

W. CASPARI: 'Tod und Auferstehung nach der Endwartung des späteren Judentumes' *Journ. of Soc. of Oriental Research*, 10 (1926), pp. 1 ff.

L. DÜRR: *Die Wertung des Lebens im A.T. und im antiken Orient* (1926).

P. KLEINERT: 'Zur Idee des Lebens im AT' ThStKr 68 (1895), pp. 693-732.

K. F. MÜLLER: *Die israelitischen Anschauungen über die Beziehungen der Toten zu den Lebenden in der Zeit des Jahvismus* (unpubl. dissertation, Kiel, 1920).

F. NÖTSCHER: *Altorientalischer und alttestamentlicher Auferstehungsglaube* (1926).

O. PROCKSCH: 'Der Lebensgedanke im A.T.' in *Christentum u. Wiss.* 4 (1928), pp. 145-158, 193-206.

G. QUELL: *Die Auffassung des Todes in Israel* (1925).

A. SCHULZ: 'Der Sinn des Todes im A.T.' (*Verzeichnis der Vorlesungen an der Akademie zu Braunsberg*, 1919).

E. SELLIN: 'Die alttestamentliche Hoffnung auf Auferstehung und ewiges Leben', *Neue kirchl. Zeitschr.* 30 (1919), pp. 232-289.

R. H. CHARLES: *A Critical History of the Doctrine of a Future Life in Israel, in Judaism and in Christianity* (1913).

A. R. JOHNSON: *The Vitality of the Individual* (1949).

T. MARSHALL: 'Life and Death (Hebrew)', *ERE* VIII (1915), 31-34.

R. MARTIN-ACHARD: *From Death to Life* (1960).

A. RICHARDSON (ed.): *A Theological Word Book of the Bible* (1950), pp. 60 f., 127 f.

H. H. ROWLEY: *The Faith of Israel* (1956), Ch. VI, and cf. footnotes for further references.

E. F. SUTCLIFFE: *The O.T. and the Future Life* (1946).

CHAPTER II

C. F. NÄGELSBACH: *Die homerische Theologie* (1840), pp. 308-350.
—— *Die nachhomerische Theologie* (1857), pp. 371-423.
W. F. OTTO: *Die Götter Griechenlands* (1929), pp. 175-191.
E. ROHDE: *Psyche* (⁴1907).
K. SAUER: *Untersuchungen zir Darstellung des Todes in der griech.-röm. Geschichtsschreibung* (Dissertation, Frankfurt, 1930).
STOBAEUS, *Eclogæ* IV, 1066-1112.
A. W. MAIR: 'Life and Death (Greek and Roman)', *ERE* VIII (1915), 25-31.
J. H. MOULTON and G. MILLIGAN: *Vocabulary of the Greek N.T.* III (1919), p. 274.

CHAPTER III

The relevant bibliographical references appear in the footnotes.

CHAPTERS IV and V

J. B. FREY: 'Le Concept de "vie" dans l'Évangile de Saint Jean', *Biblica*, 1 (1920), pp. 37-58, 211-239.
J. LINDBLOM: *Das ewige Leben* (1914).
E. VON SCHRENCK: *Die johanneische Anschauung vom 'Leben'* (1898).
F. C. BURKITT: 'Life, ζωή, ḥayyîm', *ZNW*, 12 (1911), 228-230.
W. F. COBB: 'Life and Death (Christian)', *ERE* VIII (1915), 16-19.
C. H. DODD: *The Bible and the Greeks* (1935), pp. 152 f., 161 f., 167.
D. B. LYONS: *The Concept of Eternal Life in John* (1938).
G. C. MARTIN: 'Life and Death', *HDB* III (1900), 114-119.
J. MÜLLER: *Der Lebensbegriff des hl. Pls.* (1940).
F. MUSSNER: *ZΩH* (*Joh. lit.*) (Dissertation, Munich, 1952).
J. NÉLIS: 'L'antithèse littéraire *ZΩH-ΘANATOΣ* dans les Épîtres pauliniennes', *Ephemerides Theologicae Lovanienses*, XX (1943), pp. 18-53.
E. SOMMERLATH: *Der Ursprung des neuen Lebens nach Pls.* (1940).
Reference may also be made to the general theologies of the Old and New Testaments.

ABBREVIATIONS

ANET   *Ancient Near Eastern Texts relating to the O.T.*, ed.
            J. B. Pritchard (1950).
AOT   *Altorientalische Texte zum A.T.*, ed. H. Gressmann
            (²1926).
ARW   *Archiv für Religionswissenschaft.*
CAF   *Comicorum Atticorum fragmenta*, ed. Koch (1880 ff.).
CSEL   *Corpus Scriptorum Ecclesiasticorum Latinorum*, (1866 ff.).
Diels   H. Diels, *Die Fragmente der Vorsokratiker*, ed. W. Kranz
            (I, ⁷1954; II, III, ⁶1952); cf. K. Freeman, *Ancilla to
            the PreSocratic Philosophers. A complete translation of the
            fragments in Diels* . . . (1948).
Ditt Or   W. Dittenberger, *Orientis Graeci Inscriptiones Selectae*,
            I-II (1903-5).
Ditt Syll   W. Dittenberger, *Sylloge Inscriptionum Graecarum*, I-IV,
            1, 2 (³1915-24).
DOTT   *Documents from Old Testament Times*, ed. D. Winton
            Thomas (1958).
ERE   *Encyclopaedia of Religion and Ethics*, ed. J. Hastings.
HDB   *Dictionary of the Bible*, ed. J. Hastings.
JHSt   *Journal of Hellenic Studies.*
Kautzsch   *Die Heilige Schrift des A.T.* transl. E. Kautzsch, ed. 4
            by A. Bertholet (1921 ff.).
KlT   *Kleine Texte* . . . ed. H. Lietzmann (1902 ff.).
Mas   Masoretic Text.
Pr-Bauer   E. Preuschen, *Griechisch-deutsches Wörterbuch* . . . *NT*,
            ed. W. Bauer (⁵1958). ET of ed. 4 (1949 ff.) by
            W. F. Arndt and F. W. Gingrich (1957).
RGG²   *Religion in Geschichte und Gegenwart* (²1927 ff.).
SAB   *Sitzungsberichte der Preussischen Akademie der Wissen-
            schaften zu Berlin.*
Str-B.   H. L. Strack and P. Billerbeck, *Kommentar zum NT
            aus Talmud und Midrash* (²1956).
ThStKr   *Theologische Studien und Kritiken.*
WJ   G. Dalman, *Worte Jesu* (²1930).
ZNW   *Zeitschrift für die neutestamentliche Wissenschaft.*

Works which appear in the Bibliography are referred to in the
text and footnotes by the author's name either alone or with an
abbreviated title. References to classical texts are in some cases
followed by the name of the editor whose text has been used. The
normal sigla are used for reference to Versions and manuscripts.

I. LIFE AND DEATH IN THE OLD TESTAMENT

THE ideas of life and death, in so far as they find shape in the writings of the Old Testament, are naturally related to the ideas which are common to the whole oriental world. Indeed, in many respects, they are directly dependent on ideas which the great civilisations created and gave to the neighbouring lands as already developed concepts. The religion of Yahweh, it is true, had within it forces which gave it the very considerable ability to transform even what it had taken over, to change its emphasis and to subject it to its own specific ideas. It is not our task, however, to work out the differences by a method of subtraction, but rather to ascertain the fundamental viewpoint which is characteristic of the OT, taking into consideration the entanglement of the Israelite ideas with those common to the whole oriental world. Only thus can the theologian reach the required understanding of the relevant texts.

1. *Life in the Old Testament*

The OT *ḥayyīm*[1] does not, as a concept, cover the same range of meaning as our 'life'. *Ḥayyīm* signifies only physical organic life and that, indeed, mostly as it embodies the interaction of the forces and manifestations of life.[2] Nevertheless, for the Hebrew the concept

[1] In Phoenician *ḥym*, M. Lidzbarski, *Handbuch der nordsemitischen Epigraphik* (1908), p. 273. Perhaps an abstract form.

[2] F. Delitzsch, *Biblische Psychologie* (²1861), p. 82; the verb *ḥyh* does not cover so wide a range as the abstract concept. Baudissin, p. 158. *nepeš* too is frequently a word of life; originally *nepeš* was a light breath but as the characteristic sign of life the word acquired the meaning 'life'. J. Köberle, *Natur und Geist nach der Auffassung des AT* (1901), p. 180.

is much more than the objective verification of an elemental fact. It embraces at the same time a very emphatic value-judgement; not so much because life is the first prerequisite to all possessions and aspirations, but because the possession of life in the whole OT is felt, *per se*, to be an absolutely unqualified good, in fact the highest good. Wisdom holds in her left hand wealth and honour but in her right hand long life (Prov. iii.16). *All that a man hath will he give for his life* (Job. ii.4). Only at the very extremity of despair can the Israelite go to the length of extolling death,[1] for even *a living dog is better than a dead lion.* (Eccles. ix.4). In the OT 'life' is often used simply as a word for happiness.[2] This estimate of the present possession of life, which can scarcely be surpassed, also completely dominates the thought of Egypt and Babylonia. In Israel the prolongation of physical existence to a 'ripe old age'[3] in which a man dies *an old man and full of years*[4] was, in itself, considered a particular favour and Deuteronomy, for example, occasionally offers as a reward for the observance of the divine commands nothing more nor less than long life.[5] In the same way the infinitely varied seeking for Wisdom has as its main object the achievement for man of long life.

It was likewise an idea common to the whole oriental world that the presence of the life-power was traceable to a creative act of the deity. But the more precise details of the divine origin of life received surprisingly little investigation by Israel. The Yahwist, however, does make a statement which goes beyond the general derivation of life from God when he says that God breathed the breath of life into the nostrils of the still

---

[1] Job iii.17 ff.; Ecclus. xli.2.   [2] Baudissin, p. 159.
[3] Gen. xv.15; Judges viii. 32, etc.
[4] Gen. xxv.8, xxxv.29; Job xlii.17, etc.
[5] e.g. Deut. v. 16, xvi.20, xxx.19.

lifeless man (Gen. ii.7). The author of the Priestly narrative apparently avoided formulating explicitly the divine origin of life in man. It is the very climax of all creation stories, the transmission of life, upon which he, with pious reticence, does not dare touch.[1] The seat of life for him, and this was indeed a conception held generally among the Hebrews, is the blood.[2]

Both the theologians who wrote OT creation stories take the view, though each in his own way, that after the creation life suffered a serious disruption. The author of P indicates this in the regular diminishing of the duration of life of the patriarchs. Something in man deteriorates the further he gets from his starting point in creation (Gen. v). The Yahwist sees in this shortening of the duration of life the imposition of divine punishment (Gen. vi.3); this limitation in time is thus connected very closely with human sin. The important question whether in fact, according to the Yahwist, the limitation of human life first took place at the fall is probably to be answered in the negative. The decree of the fate of death is never expressed;[3] the

---

[1] Although for him the creation simply by means of the word is of primary significance, yet he does not assert that creation of life is by means of the word; here certainly he was still too closely bound to older thought forms. Whereas for the plants and beasts it appears to sound like the Mother Earth concept (*tōṣē' hā'āreṣ*), for man there is no statement at all.

[2] Gen. ix.4; Lev. xvii.14. There seems indeed to be a certain contradiction between this and the other view which considers the breath as the constitutive element of life.

[3] Death is only mentioned in the subordinate clause (iii. 19b). If the curse had been meant to inflict death on those who had, hitherto, been immortal, this would undoubtedly have been its main point, and certainly would not have been expressed in an accidental subordinate clause. Also the death would have then been inflicted only on the man. Gen. ii.17 is a threat which has not been carried out; it puts the death that was immediately threatened into the future (*bᵉyōm 'ᵃkolᵉkā*).

purport of the curse was not death but life and its embitterment. Thus the OT knows nothing of death as being in itself the wages of sin. Only an early or dishonourable death, or one that is extraordinary in some way, is reckoned as punishment. However, the Yahwist traces two changes for the worse in natural life to the fall; the pain of childbirth and the sense of shame between the two sexes. It must, however, be noted that the Yahwist in these reflections is, as elsewhere, alone among the OT witnesses. The same is true of the parallel narrative of the tree of life—inserted in the story of paradise and the fall[1]—whose fruit could have given man immortality if God had not expelled him from the garden. The connection with a myth common to the whole oriental world is indisputable. Even apart from this there are manifold suggestions of such originally mythical elements in the OT, but when the fountain of life and the water of life are mentioned it is a question only of figurative speech. The mythical background is completely forgotten and in fact supplanted by the idea, theologically extremely significant, of a quite different factor on which life depends and to which it is subjected.

In Israel men evidently occupied themselves theologically very little with the primeval history of life. They knew about the ultimate source,[2] but very much more important for the living person was the immediate fact of his absolute dependence on God. God is Lord over life and death,[3] he keeps the book of life.[4] Since

---

[1] cf. *SIN* (1951) in this series, pp. 23 ff. The central narrative is concerned with the tree of knowledge. For the interwoven tradition of the tree of life consult the commentaries.

[2] Ps. xxxvi.9 [Heb. 10], cxxxix.13 ff.

[3] Num.xxvii. 16; Job xii.10; Deut. xxxii.39.

[4] The concept of the book of Life is, however, a double one. One concept refers to a book of fate already in heaven, Exod.

he was for Israel the one who had given the people its covenant, the conclusion was automatically reached that the preservation or loss of life is decided by one's attitude to his word. Now this belief embraces the most important distinctive feature of the OT view of life. The Israelite did not build his view of life on an elaborate mythology; he does not seek contact with the creative life by means of magic rites or in mysteries;[1] but rather the word of God placed him at a point of decision between life and death. This idea is expounded with such insistence that, as a result, the story of the origin of things and the statements about the bestowal of life are almost emptied of content. The creative implantation of life is bound to be of less importance for the person who knows that its immediate possession or loss depends only on the word of God and who thus, as it were, is brought by life itself once more face to face with the possibility of grace. With the promulgation of Deuteronomy, Moses sets life and death before Israel (Deut. xxx.15-20) and Israel is to choose life *for it is no vain thing for you, for it is your life* (Deut. xxxii.47). Thus Deuteronomy, which presents this idea in constantly changing variations, arrives at the paradoxical formulation that man's physical existence is dependent not only on bread but on the word of God (Deut. viii.3).

This view, however, is by no means specifically Deuteronomic. Amos already considered the possibility

xxxii.32; Mal. iii.16; Ps. lxix.28 [Heb. 29] which has in it something of the idea of predestination. The other speaks of a list of citizens which is kept in the temporal or eschatological community (Isa. iv.3).

[1] cf. examples of rites intended to restore life in those who are ill; E. Ebling, *Tod und Leben nach den Vorstellungen der Babylonier* (1931), pp. 65 ff.; for the Osiris Mysteries in Egypt cf. H. Kees, *Totenglauben und Jenseitsvorstellungen der alten Ägypter* (1926), pp. 348 ff.

that a hunger for God's word would trouble men and lay them low (Amos viii.11 ff.). But none of those whose sayings have come down to us has worked out this idea as uncompromisingly as Ezekiel. In broad, dogmatic statements he frees life from all false supports and connections and makes it completely dependent on the word of God.[1] The obedient man chooses for himself life, the disobedient man death. The whole of the discussion results in the one straightforward idea, not that the righteous man receives, for example, special gifts of grace, but that he remains alive while the disobedient man has to die. Ezekiel evidently assumes a speedy death for the sinner. Here the connecting of the natural process of life to the word of God is complete and the theological consequence of this is plain: Israel should, as a matter of principle, have understood natural life in terms of grace. It is for him not only an expression of the state of grace but is the most elementary basis of the state of grace. Only by faith, i.e. by clinging to the God of salvation, will the righteous man have life.[2] It is clear that life is here seen totally as a gift, indeed— and here we meet the evaluation common to the whole oriental world in a newly emphasised form—as a thing enjoyed;[3] partly the enjoyment of all kinds of material goods which are seen as the blessing of Yahweh, and partly of communion with God, the unshakeable security of which makes the godly man blessed.[4]

[1] Ezek. iii.18 ff., xiv.13 ff., xviii.1 ff., xx. 1 ff., xxxiii.1 ff.
[2] Hab. ii.4, cf. Amos. v.4, 14; Jer. xxxviii.20.
[3] Kleinert, pp. 720 ff. This gives the meaning of I Kings iii. 5 ff. What is praised is not the fact that Solomon objectively valued wisdom above life but his selflessness, which renounced such a great individual blessing in the interests of the people who were to be governed.
[4] We occasionally also find statements from the pious in the OT which have a slight mystical colouring. Cf. Ps. xxxvi.9 f. [Heb. 10], lxxiii. 25, xvi.11.

OT Wisdom has, for all the many ways in which she woos men, only one basic aim, to offer life to man, or, in her favourite expression, to lead him in *the path of life*.[1] Here also, therefore, the possession and preservation of life cannot be taken for granted as something in itself automatic but rather it is bound to a spiritual and religious system. In fact it is fundamentally by this that possession or loss of life is decided. Nevertheless a not inconsiderable theological change has taken place here, one which finds expression in a certain disintegration of the strict OT concept of revelation. It is not God, nor the word of God, nor his law, but wisdom,[2] in fact the words of the wise [3] and discipline [4] that give life. The ways of folly lead to death.[5] A psalmist could still praise Yahweh as the fountain of life (Ps. xxxvi.9 [Heb. 10]), but in the realm of the *Ḥokmā* (Wisdom) literature this metaphor, which has lost its significance in the mythical sense, is applied to wisdom.[6] The difference from the way in which Deuteronomy or the prophets, for example, understood the dependence of life is plain; it is connected with the theologising of wisdom which became placed between God and man as an intermediate entity with a strong revelatory content.

---

[1] Prov. ii.19, v.6, vi.23, x.17, xv.24. The idea, first in Jer. xxi. 8, is only remotely like that sometimes found in ancient oriental literature; the evidence in A. Jirku, *Altorientalischer Komm. zum AT* (1923), p. 205 (on Jer. xxi. 8); more important is the fact that in Egyptian wisdom literature also there is this desire to acquire life; cf. the wisdom of Amenemope AOT, pp. 38 ff.; ANET, pp. 421 ff.; DOTT, pp. 172 ff.

[2] Prov. iii.16, 18, viii.35, ix. 11.

[3] Prov. iii.2, iv.4, 10, 22, xiii.14, xix.16.

[4] Prov. iv.13, vi.23, x.17, xxiii.14.

[5] How far in such statements life and death are to be understood spiritually so that here already there is a feeling after the idea of a death without a physical death (Sellin, p. 270) is very questionable. One must be cautious on this point.

[6] Prov. xiii.14, xvi.22; Ecclus. xxi.13.

Both Ezekiel, who took the prophetic idea of life's dependence on God to its remorseless conclusion, and the teachers of wisdom with their theory, brought themselves into a serious conflict with normal observation and daily experience, which is an important indication of what unyielding dogmatic interests were present in their thinking. This conflict was in fact realised [1] but it was only reconciled when Israel no longer looked on death definitely as the irrevocable end of life.

2. Death in the Old Testament

The evaluation of death within the religion of Yahweh is as uniform and as unvarying as the way of seeing Yahweh's relation to life was manifold and theologically various, even over many centuries of eventful religious development. The limitation of life by (normal, late) death is seen, it is true, as something extremely lamentable, but it is nevertheless taken simply for granted [2] as something against which one does not revolt. Thus the godly man of the OT meets the absolutely irrevocable ordinance of death in perfect resignation.[3] The existence that awaits him, a joyless shadowy existence, is in no way whatever comparable to even the most wretched life on earth. Nowhere does even the idea of reunion cheer the gloom of this expectation.[4] The grave is the abode of the dead man, strictly speaking for an unlimited duration, although practically speaking, it is true, the subsequent removal

---

[1] Ps. xlix.8 ff., lxxiii.2 ff., xcii.7 f. [Heb. 8 f.]; Job xxi.7.

[2] II Sam. xiv.14: *For we must needs die, and are as water spilt on the ground, which cannot be gathered up again.*

[3] Job vii.9; Ps. lxxxix.48 [Heb. 49]. Even the pre-apocalyptic visions of the end-time do not envisage the abolition of death but at the most an extension of the span of life. Isa. lxv. 20; Zech. viii.4.

[4] Quell, p. 31.

of the remains of the body from its resting place into the pit, where they mixed with the remains of other corpses, signified for the survivors the surrender of the last vestiges of individuality and separate existence of the dead person.

The idea of a realm of the dead in the cosmic depths, Sheol, the common assembly ground of all the dead, exists side by side with the above idea, but curiously without the two being reconciled. This second concept, though no less gloomy, is evidently of different origin from the notion of the shadowy existence in the sepulchral chamber. In the OT it is found mostly in poetic works.

There is no need to mention here the admittedly polymorphous ideas that lay behind the various rites and burial customs. In mourning and similar rites elements that are quite primitive and very heterogeneous are usually preserved. They become combined with one another, are changed and become filled with new content, so that it is extremely difficult to discern the meaning given to them at a particular time. The important thing, however, is this: that where they are still in vogue with an active religious force they are for the most part bitterly opposed by the religion of Yahweh.[1] Even if a certain numinous fear, nourished by earlier stages of religion, can be detected in Israel, nevertheless in its legitimate religion all positive holy quality was denied the grave, corpse and spirit of the dead man.[2] The dead person is unclean and makes others unclean.[3] In this the strongest possible cultic rejection is expressed. If, therefore, the denial of an individual numinous significance to the dead person

---

[1] Lev. xix.31, xx.6, 27; Deut. xviii.11, xxvi.14, xiv.1.

[2] The rites that are permitted within the Israelite religion are all separated from their primitive cultic meanings (tearing of clothes, cutting of hair, etc.).   [3] Num. xix.16; Deut. xxi.23.

and the grave is quite obvious, the question of the relation between Yahweh and the dead and their realm nevertheless leads to a very strange conclusion.

The complaint, uttered in various contexts that the dead person is excluded from the praise of God takes us to the core of the concept that is dominant here. *The earth he hath given to the children of men. The dead praise not Yahweh.*[1] After death, therefore, the godly man stands beyond the realm of life, which was infinitely precious to him and in which is maintained the cultic relation to Yahweh. Another supplicant draws the consequences still more clearly. Isa. xxxviii.18: *For the grave* (Sheol) *cannot praise thee, death cannot celebrate thee; they that go down to the pit cannot hope for thy truth.* Yahweh's faithfulness *'emet* has become meaningless for the dead. This means, then, quite simply *they are cut off from thy hand.*[2] It is really here that the actual sting, which death had for OT religion through the centuries, resides. Yahweh is the god of life in a quite exclusive sense. The sharp contrast to the notion of Yahweh's relation to life is equally clear. We saw above how life was not only given by Yahweh physically but its preservation was also acknowledged as being dependent on God as a result of his own decision. Thus while we saw that it was precisely life's connection with God that was absolute, here it is the absence of such a connection that is

[1] Ps. cxv.16 f. [Heb. 17]; also Isa. xxxviii.11; Ps. vi.5 [Heb. 6], xxx.9 [Heb. 10], lxxxviii.10 ff. [Heb. 11 ff.]; Ecclus. xvii.27.

[2] Ps. lxxxviii.5 [Heb. 6]. Only twice in the OT are these concepts overcome. In Amos ix.2 and Ps. cxxxix.8, God's power extends even to Sheol. Both these claims do not reproduce the usual idea but are the conclusion drawn from an individual act of faith in the power of Yahweh. The idea of being taken up to another life was popular; but it does not refer to an intervention of Yahweh in Sheol but to being taken away immediately on death, at the end of life.

characteristic. Death and its realm stand outside the stream of power which has subdued all areas of life, and the absence of a theological point of orientation for the concepts of the state of death resulted in the fact that, within the Yahwistic faith, these have been preserved in an undecided and unreconciled state not otherwise found in the OT. The question whether the dead person rests with his 'fathers' in the family grave (e.g. Gen. l.13; Josh. xxiv.32; I Kings ii.10, xi.43), or in Sheol amongst princes, generals and peoples (Isa. xiv.9 ff.; Ezek. xxxii.21 ff.), remained open. Within the Yahwistic faith there arose no inducement to unify this and similar differences.

The explanation of these surprising findings, from the point of view of the history of religion, will have to be sought in the fact that, of all areas of the previously non-Yahwistic cultus, that of death remained longest unfused into the legitimate religion. As long as the religious powers of Israel were engaged in such a persistent struggle with the cult of the dead—that is as long as this area was devalued by it religiously—it also resisted a positive incorporation into the religion of Yahweh. Of course the Yahweh religion would have had a quite different approach at this obscure point if it had not in fact had in its possession, right from the beginning, an important religious equivalent. The people was assured of permanence and continuance beyond the transience of the individual in the idea of the covenant, and Ezekiel's mighty vision in chapter xxxvii shows how faith was indeed in a position to look forward to a return of the people even from the most wretched state of death.[1]

---

[1] Similarly Hos. vi. 2, xiii.14. Concerning the allusion to the Adonis cult, cf. Sellin, pp. 247 f. Also the hope of perpetuating the name from generation to generation was a compensation (Isa. lxvi.22; Ps. lxxii.17).

3. *The conquest of death in the Old Testament*

It still remains to be shown at what point the curse that death had laid on the individual life was broken. Although the statements that belong here have little relevance to the central religious concern, it is nevertheless important to recognise from what forces this last inference drew its nourishment. The idea that God is still in control of higher realms of life, into which as a rule no man can penetrate but into which, in quite rare and exceptional cases, God might carry off (technical term in Hebrew *lāqaḥ*) a chosen individual, was probably common to the whole Israelite world.[1] However, there was no 'development' from this idea of a speculative concept of resurrection and eternal life, but individual godly men, when in grave agonies about their faith, fell back on it as a possibility that could be expected of God.

It was above all the question of Yahweh's justice and thus of the ultimate realisation of his covenant promise which pressed them towards a solution beyond death. In Psalm xvi nothing is said either of resurrection or of being 'taken' or of similar happenings but one can see clearly to what conclusions clinging to Yahweh's mercy could lead. *My heart is glad . . . For thou wilt not leave my soul to Sheol; neither wilt thou suffer thy holy one to see corruption* (*the pit*. Ps. xvi.9 f.). The author of Psalm xlix expresses his hope even more clearly and boldly. *God will redeem my soul from the power of Sheol; for he shall receive me* (Ps. xlix.15 [Heb. 16]). Even to this godly man this hope came under the compulsion of the problem of theodicy. Yahweh's promise cannot fail. He is the *pōdeh*, the liberating deliverer who will take up the cause of him who is in need. Job xix.25

---

[1] Gen. v.21 ff.: Enoch; II Kings ii.9 f.: Elijah; Isa. liii.8: the Servant.

points in precisely the same direction. Here God is the *gō'ēl* from whom, because he has taken up his cause, Job expects deliverance (though after death).[1] This certainty of continuing the relationship founded on grace and of the indestructability of the fellowship started by God is in Psalm lxxiii expressed with wonderful clarity. *Nevertheless I am continually with thee. . . . Thou shalt guide me with thy counsel and afterwards receive me to glory.* [Unless we should here read *'ōraḥ, path* for *'aḥar, after,* i.e. *lead me in a glorious path*—ed.] *Whom have I in heaven but thee . . . my flesh and my heart faileth, but God is the strength of my heart and my portion for ever* (Ps. lxxiii.23-26). It could be said that the OT belief in a life after death was formulated here in its clearest form. Absolutely unmagical, unmythical, unspeculative even unmystical, this prospect is a conviction which presented itself to the godly man from the idea of grace alone and from nothing else.

Less as an individual venture of faith but nevertheless as a proclamation of grace there is the assurance for Israel in the apocalyptic passage in Isaiah. *Thy dead shall live; thy bodies shall rise* (Isa. xxvi.19). Theologically this hope is on a completely different footing. Here it is a question of a conviction which suddenly introduces an entirely new perspective into the great framework of Israel's eschatology. Related to it is the prospect which is presented at the end of the book of Daniel. *And many of them that sleep in the dust of the earth shall awake, some to everlasting life and some to shame and everlasting contempt* (Dan. xii.2). Here the new element is the resurrection not only of those who still have to receive Yahweh's grace but also the resurrection to judgement of those condemned. By this time we have an essentially new view before us. The survival of death is not a

---

[1] So most commentators. For Yahweh as *gō'ēl*, cf. Gen. xlviii. 16; Jer. l.34; Ps. cxix.154; Prov. xxiii.11.

conviction that comes to him that clings to Yahweh but
only one element in a comprehensive eschatology which
is passed on as an idea already fully worked out in all
essential features. Here are finally abandoned the
classic and ancient Hebrew view of life in this present
world—a life, which through the absence of all hope in
a world beyond, had laid upon man an absolutely inescapable religious demand—and also the solution of
the problem of death in a personal venture of faith, of
which there is an occasional hint in the Psalter.

4. *The Old Testament concept of life*

The OT understanding of life cannot be deduced
alone from the use of *hayyim* (*hāyāh*), even if this does
show a characteristic side of the concept. The phenomenon of natural life, whose subject is primarily man,
is not made the object of scientific observation and
reflection in the OT, and is not conceived primarily as
a phenomenon of nature. It is the being which man
himself is, and above all his existence in time. 'Life'
and 'days (of life)' can be used synonymously and,
when life is aspired after, desired or promised, what is
intended first and foremost is that existence should
have duration.[1] Even where the concept of life is
orientated by means of its opposite concept death, the
fact emerges that life has a dimension in time whose
end is death. Death itself, also, is not contemplated
as a natural occurrence; it is the end and the idea
that life and death can be conceived in a dialectic
unity is out of the question. To this extent *hayyim*

---

[1] cf. E.von Schrenck, pp. 3-11; J. Lindblom, pp. 1-47; and especially L. Dürr, pp. 2-11. These give the evidence that the subject
of life as a span can also be the community. According to F. C.
Burkitt, ZNW, 12 (1911), pp. 228-30, the plural *hayyim* could be
understood to mean that life is thought of as the succession of
temporal moments.

corresponds more to the Greek βίος [inasmuch as this means not the manner in which life is led but its duration (cf. p. 23)], than to the Greek ζωή. *Ζωή* corresponds rather to the Hebrew *nepeš* in so far as *nepeš* means the power on which life is based[1]: it is the actual subject of living and dying.[2] Thus every living thing can be described as *kol-hannepeš*.[3] 'Life' and 'soul' can stand together in a parallel [4] and *nepeš* can be used to mean the 'ego', the 'self' (Judges xvi.30; I Sam. xviii.3). It is this self that is alive.[5]

As the concept *ḥayyīm* denotes the extent of existence in time, so to the same extent the essence of this living existence itself is seen in the manifestations of life whose subject is the *nepeš*. These are the vital manifestations of life such as hunger and thirst, desires and wishes, love and hate.[6] *Nepeš*, unlike the Greek ψυχή, is not the subject of spiritual life.[7] This is seen in the way in which the concept of life is also connected with the concept of flesh.[8] *Bāśār* is that which is alive [9] and all

---

[1] *Nepeš* often corresponds more to the Greek ζῷον (Gen. ii. 7, etc.) and is often used in a collective meaning (J. Pedersen, *Israel, its life and culture* (1926), pp. 99-181). The individual living creatures live in mutual dependence and connection but this connection is more to be understood historically than cosmically; it is before all else that of the family and the people (*ibid.* pp. 255-259, 474-476) and the Covenant (*ibid.* pp. 308 f.).

[2] Gen. xxxv.18; Judges xvi.30; II Sam. i.9; Ezek. xiii.19.

[3] Josh. x.28 ff. With the addition *ḥayyāh* Gen. i.21, 24, ix. 10 ff.; Lev. xi.10.

[4] Ps. lxxviii.50, lxxxviii.3 [Heb. 4], cxliii.3; Job xxxiii.18, 22, 28, xxxvi.14, cf. Pedersen, *op. cit.* pp. 151-156.

[5] cf. the oath formula, I Sam. i.26, xvii.55.

[6] cf. B. Stade, *Biblische Theologie des AT*, I (1905), p. 181. Pedersen, *op. cit.*, pp. 100 f., 147.

[7] cf. TWNT III, pp. 609 ff., IV, pp. 950 ff.

[8] Pedersen, *op. cit.* pp. 176-179. The OT does not distinguish at all between animate and inanimate creation. All that exists in nature is thought of as living (*ibid.* pp. 155, 479-482).

[9] Ezek. xi. 19, xxxvi. 26.

human beings or all living creatures can be described
as *kol-bāśār*.[1] 'Soul' and 'flesh' can be used as parallels
or combined.[2] Indeed occasionally *bāśār* can almost
mean 'self'.[3]

If *nepeš* is occasionally seen as a 'something' which is
to be found in man or in his blood [4], this statement
again is not to be understood in terms of objective
investigation, but, in that it is based on primitive
observation, what is expressed in it is the thought of the
transcendent nature of life and that it is not given into
the hands of man. This emerges especially in the passages
which say that man lives because God has given him
the breath of life (*nišmat-ḥayyīm*) [5] or that *rūaḥ*, which is
controlled by God alone,[6] dwells in him, so that
'flesh' as something human and 'spirit' as something
divine can in fact appear in contrast (Isa. xxxi.3; cf.
Ps. lxxviii.39).[7] Man possesses life therefore only, as
it were, as something on loan.[8] God is lord over life;[9]
he is the 'living one' (Deut. v.26 [Heb. 23]; II Kings
xix.4; Ps. xlii.2 [Heb. 3]);[10] he is the fountain of life
(Ps. xxxvi.9 [Heb. 10]); he kills and makes alive (Deut.
xxxii.39). He has life within himself whilst man has to
maintain his own life through his nourishment and

---

[1] Gen. vi.12 ff., 19, vii.16, 21.

[2] Ps. xvi.9 f., lxiii.1 [Heb. 2], lxxxiv.2 [Heb. 3], Job. xiii.14.

[3] Prov. xiv.30; Eccles. iv.5, v.6 [Heb. 5], xi.10, xii.12.

[4] Gen. ix.4; Lev. xvii.11, 14; Deut. xii.23.

[5] Gen. ii.7; cf. Num. xxvii.16; Job. xii.10.

[6] Gen. vi.3, 17, vii.15, 22; Num. xvi.22; Ps. civ.29 f.; Job. xxxiv.14 f.

[7] It is not meant dualistically; cf. Pedersen, *op. cit.* p. 146;
on body and soul, *ibid.*, pp. 170-179.

[8] So that *ḥyym* almost never takes a genitive of the possessor.
Baudissin, p. 157, n. 1.

[9] cf. esp. Ps. civ.29 f.; Job xxxiv.14 f.

[10] Kleinert, pp. 630 ff.

[11] Deut. viii.3; II Kings iv.7; Gen. xxvii.40. Also life equals
food, Prov. xxvii.27.

livelihood [11] if God does not maintain it for him miraculously (Deut. viii.3). Man is mortal.[1]

The ideas that life extends in time and that it is realised in the vital manifestations of life, belong together in the unity of a concept of life. If 'life' is most commonly characterised as movement,[2] then it can be described more exactly as having aims, as having potentialities, as being skilled at something or as having the desire and ability to achieve something.[3] As hunger and thirst, desiring and wishing and the like are expressions of the *nepeš*, being desirous, zealous or hopeful are similarly characteristics of life.[4] Mere existence is not in itself life, so that the shadowy continuance of existence in Sheol is not considered life (Eccles. ix.4). A life whose potentialities are taken away is no longer life. Illness is as bad as death (Job xxvii.15). To recover and to live are the same thing.[5] Thus God's life also has its reality in that he acts and creates.[6] As 'to live' can be used to mean 'to live a long time' it can also mean 'to live happily'.[7] Life acquires simply the meaning of happiness.[8] Since he who is alive still has hopes and desires, life is considered the highest good of all.[9] Death is only welcome to the desperate man (Job iii.11-26); the greatest suffering is

---

[1] Gen. iii.19; II Sam. xiv.14; Isa. xl.6; Ps. lxxviii.39, lxxxix.48 [Heb. 49]; xc.

[2] Gen. vii.21; cf. Gen. i.28, viii.19; Ps. lxix.34 [Heb. 35]; flowing water is 'living' water.   [3] Pedersen, *op. cit.* pp. 147, 152 f.

[4] Job xxxiii.20, xxxviii.39; Eccles. ix.4, 6, 10.

[5] Baudissin, p. 152. In so far as life is manifested in living activity, death is not just an end; it is indeed the end, but as a power which is constantly threatening and inhibiting life. Pedersen, *op. cit.* pp. 153, 180 f., 466-470.

[6] Josh. iii. 10 f.; I Sam. xvii. 26; II Kings xix.4; Jer. x.10-16.

[7] cf. the desire in Ps. lxix.33 [Heb. 34], xxii.26 [Heb. 27].

[8] Baudissin, pp. 143 ff. Pedersen, *op. cit.* pp. 154 f.

[9] I Kings iii.11; Prov. iii.16; Job ii.4.

suffering 'unto death' (Jonah iv.9). The possibility of seeing death as an act, and, consequently, as the extreme fulfilment of life is, like suicide, nowhere envisaged (cf. p. 8); i.e. death is only viewed as the threatened or actual end of life, or as the state of being dead, not as the act of dying.

The living person is aware of himself (Eccles. ix.5); i.e. it is part of life that one understands oneself in one's own world—thus the connection of life and light.[1] Death is darkness (Eccles. xi.8); it makes everything incomprehensible (Eccles. ii. 14 ff.). Life is particular to each individual [2] and thus, as such, each life is different from the other whilst death makes everything alike (Job iii.19). But the individuality of life is basic and is not achieved by the way in which life is lived. Thus in the OT the Greek idea of the βίος, of its norm and particular potentialities, is not developed (cf. p. 23). For that reason the period of life can be described as happy or unhappy (Ps. xc.10), but it is impossible to talk of living 'happily' or 'unhappily' or of living 'well' or 'badly'.[3] Although the idea that life is an individual possession is essential to its nature, the idea of an intrinsic value which is to be gained apart from the present observable living of life is inevitably absent. Death, therefore, finally poses the question whether life with all its joys and troubles and despite all its variation is not vain because all ultimately suffer one fate, all have to die.[4] In general, of course, death can

---

[1] Ps. xxvii.1, xxxvi.9 [Heb. 10]; Job iii.20, xxxiii.28, 30; Eccles. xi.7 f. Cf. Pedersen, *op. cit.* pp. 313, 464-466. Cf. also the hymn to the sun of Akhenaten in A. Erman, *Die Literatur der Ägypter* (1923), pp. 358-363; G. Roeder, *Urkunden zur Religion des alten Ägypten* (1923), pp. 62-65; AOT, pp. 15-18; ANET, pp. 369 ff., DOTT, pp. 142 ff.

[2] Pedersen, *op. cit.* pp. 100-103. The soul has always an individual character.   [3] Baudissin, pp. 157 f.

[4] Eccles. ii.14-17, iii.19-21, viii.10, ix.2 f.

be seen as well-earned rest, as sleep (Job iii.17, etc.), and man is satisfied if he dies old and full of days, if he has had a long and happy life and is then *gathered unto his fathers*.[1] We are far away from the idea that such a life cannot have value. In the OT life is talked about neither in the idealistic nor the dualistic sense. As bodily life, in time, it has its intrinsic value if it is long and happy.[2] This possibility is put into the hands of man in so far as he acquires a long and happy life by his obedience under God's law and the decrees of wisdom, or earns death by his disobedience,[3] so that the choice between the way of life and the way of death is open to him.[4]

[1] Pedersen, *op. cit.* pp. 327 f., 495 f.

[2] Pedersen, *op. cit.* pp. 147 f.; the soul must be filled, satisfied. To a full life strength, happiness, health, length of days also belong, *ibid.* pp. 230, 313-316, 327-329.

[3] Deut. xxx.15-20, xxxii.47; Ezek. iii.18 ff., xviii.1 ff., etc., cf. Dürr, pp. 5-11. Wisdom is the 'tree of life'. Prov. iii.18.

[4] Ps. xvi.11; Prov. v.6, vi.23, x.17, xiv.12.

II. THE GREEK BACKGROUND

1. *Life*

i. *Classical usage*

(a) Ζωή (ζῆν) means in Greek the physical life of organic beings, animals and men, or even plants. Life is not regarded as a thing, but as being alive, as the quality that is characteristic of all living beings as such;[1] that is why ζωή cannot be used in the plural. Moreover, ζωή is revealed in the fact that living beings move and each has its own particular function. It is therefore possible to speak in a derivative sense of the life of, e.g. the customs in force (Soph. *Antig.* 457), and Plato can describe the word of knowledge, which can defend itself, as living and having a soul (*Phaedr.* 276a). The whole world, too, as endowed with a soul, can be called a ζῷον. The most general definition of ζωή is as movement in the widest sense—i.e. not only as movement from place to place, but as change, and particularly as self-movement in distinction from mechanical movement.

(b) In establishing this definition, however, we come to see that Greek thought originally understood something different from, and wider than, what is expressed

---

[1] Because ζωή is the essential nature of man, something that belongs to his very existence, not something that comes in to establish his status, or that just happens to him, or that varies in degree, it is never, like φύσις, θάνατος or ὑγίεια hypostatised or thought of as a divine figure. ζωή is never represented in Greek art. Even the later theological reflections of 'Orphism' (Kern, *Orph. Fr.* 298) and Stoicism (von Arnim, II, 305, 20 f.; 312, 21 f.; 315, 5; Cornutus *Theol. Graec.* 2, pp. 3, 5 ff. [ed. C. Lang, 1881]) derived the name Zeus from ζῆν etymologically (Cornutus: The soul of the world is called Zeus), but never produced a statue of ζωή.

in the scientific concept of ζωή, in which ζωή is applied in essentially the same way to men as to animals and plants. When the ζωή of the Deity is described as thought, or as contemplation, or is characterised as the best life, or blessedness, the concept of ζωή underlying this language is drawn from something that man regards as his highest potentiality, that which is characteristic of his nature, namely contemplation. Of course, in so far as thought and contemplation are thought of merely as a power present in a natural phenomenon, just like perception and ´ movement (Aristot. *An.* II.2, p. 413a. 22 ff.), they can be understood as an expression of ζωή regarded merely as a natural phenomenon. But a real understanding of mind leads beyond this; it can be described as that element which is different from biological ζωή and has come into the soul from outside (Aristot. *Gen. An.* p. 736b, 27 f.; 744b, 21), constituting the divine element in man. If the title of the mind, contemplation, is the highest and truest potentiality of man, and if such contemplation is never realised by man except in the body, and yet is as emancipated from it as possible, then the truly human ζωή is not really the same ζωή in virtue of which a being becomes a ζῷον through the union of body and soul. It thus becomes clear that in the Greek concept of ζωή, just as in that of the soul, two motifs are interwoven. For the soul (ψυχή) is on the one hand the biological principle of life in matter, and on the other hand the specifically human principle of consciousness, so that from one aspect of the Greek outlook the soul can stand in dualistic opposition to the body and can be looked upon as pre-existent and eternal, a stranger in the body. In the same way, ζωή is not only the life of the natural phenomenon, but also the specifically human life which is not simply that which man has qua ζῷον.

No clear terminological distinction in this matter was ever reached in Greek. It is, nevertheless, quite clear that life in its specifically human form must be distinguished from natural ζωή, and that this goes beyond the mere differentiation of ζωή in the different ζῷα based on the fact that not all organisms are equally rich and complex. There is this specific distinction between human and any other form of life, that its possibilities are not always actually realised, as are those of organic nature. One sign of this is that the life of man can be a life for something, in the dative (e.g. one's country, Demosth. *Or.* 7.17), whereas the purpose of natural life is the preservation of the individual ζῷον or the species. Above all, the life of man is not a state of being but an existence whose possibilities are unrealised, or at any rate only sometimes realised, whereas the life of the deity is always realised. Man is concerned about the reality of his life and, as a rule, his true life is not identical with his actual life. This can already be seen in Homer, when he speaks of 'the gods who live at ease' (*Il.* 6.138) and contrasts men 'such as mortals are now' with the heroes. We can see it also in the way in which human ζωή can be described as 'good' (Plat. *Resp.* 521a), 'most good' (Aristot. *Metaph.* XI.7, 1072b, 28), 'blessed' (Plat. *Leg.* IV.713c), 'most profitable' (Plat. *Resp.* 344e), or, on the other hand, as 'base' (Plat. *Leg.* XII.944c). It comes out most clearly of all in adverbial phrases like to live 'well', to live 'a nobler and straighter life' (Plat. *Menex.* 248d), to live 'best' (*ibid.* 248a, cf. *Gorg.* 512e), to live 'temperately' or 'rationally' (Plat. *Leg.* III.689d). This all goes to show that human life is not a natural process of nurture, growth and decay, but has in every instance its own appointed destiny, in which it finds itself happy or unhappy, as the case may be. Being aware of life's possibilities, we cannot escape from the question how truly we are living, whether our life is being rightly or wrongly spent. The expression 'to live rationally' shows that it is possible so to live (cf. Xen. *Mem.* III.3, 11). We may, indeed, come to doubt whether the life we are leading really deserves the name at all.

(c) Finally this view finds expression in the fact that, alongside of ζωή (ζῆν) we have the word βίος (βιοῦν).[1] In actual fact human life always takes shape in an individual βίος, in which it can succeed or fail, and the question arises, in what sort of βίος the ζωή of man is truly seen. *Bίος* indicates the way of life, the character, and is closely related to ἦθος.[2] It is, of course, also possible to speak of the βίος of animals and gods (Plat. *Phaedr.* 248a), but we are then thinking of the βίος of the species, whereas the βίοι of men (and here we can use the plural) are the ways in which individual lives find expression. The Greeks, of course, take it for granted that the possibilities of our βίος are limited and that the βίος of the species man finds its true expression in the right kind of βίος.[3] Accordingly βίος often becomes a technical term for a literary biography. With reference to an individual life it often means its period or length. It is possible to say βίον ζῆν for 'to live a life'. Thus ζῆν and βιοῦν are often used as synonyms, as indeed are ζωή and βίος. *Bίος* can indeed be used of the conduct of life in the external sense of calling, profession, or even livelihood or means; but

---

[1] *Bίος* and ζωή (ζῆν) are etymologically related; cf. Walde-Pokorny, I, pp. 668 f., 670. That is why their meanings overlap. But βίος and ζῆν had become so completely separated that their etymological connection had been lost. Hence in later Greek the conjugation ζῆν, ζήσομαι, ἔζησα instead of ζῆν, βιώσομαι, ἐβίων.

[2] The βιολόγος (or ἠθολόγος) is not the 'biologist', but the man who represents character, the actor.

[3] For the principles underlying the ancient concept of βίος as 'the form of life', see W. Jaeger, 'Über Ursprung und Kreislauf des philosophischen Lebensideals', SAB (1928), pp. 390 ff.

above all it means the individual life, grasped in the making of choices, open to the question of its reality, a question which finds expression in discussion whether life is worth living (Plat. *Ap.* 38a) or of the saving principle of life (Plat. *Prot.* 356d,e) or the complete life (Aristot. *Eth. Nic.* I.6, p. 1098a, 18). The answer is found in such assertions as that only life in a city is worth living. That is why the βίος of men is ruled by law (Democr. fr. 248 [II.110, 3 ff., Diels]; Plat. *Leg.* II.663a; VII.803a) and education is necessary (Plat. *Prot.* 326b; cf. also *Tim.* 44c). In the idealist philosophy life becomes real as the life of thought, of contemplation, as the life of the philosopher. Plato (*Phileb.* 22a) distinguishes three lives as the basic possibilities offered to man, and from Aristotle (*Eth. Nic.* I.3, p. 1095b, 14 ff.) onward it is usual to divide βίοι into the three classes of the life of pleasure, the life of activity (or politics) and the life of contemplation; the third is the highest, for it is the divine life (Aristot. *Eth. Nic.* X.8, p. 1178b, 20 ff.; *Metaph.* XI. 9, p. 1074b, 25 f.).

Since, then, it is inherent in the ζωή of man that it is a βίος, human life is always thought of as 'my' life. At the same time, this idea of it as 'always mine' is not thoroughly worked out. The different βίοι are not seen in their unique individuality, but are divided into similar, constantly repeated types and graded, the governing principle in this being the standard βίος. What gives each particular man his opportunity for real existence is not the historic moment and the challenge (of a 'thou') which it brings him, but the non-temporal, the universal, which he has to realise in his individual existence, it may be the law of the city, or the principle of reason. It is on this that the Greek idea of education rests. Likewise, in so far as ζωή is understood as a natural phenomenon, as, for instance, when it achieves realisation in the individual βίος as (in Platonic terms) ἀληθῶς ζῆν, it is something belonging to this world. As a mere state of being alive it does, of course, transcend the individual, but this does not make it 'other-worldly' in the religious sense. Since ζωή comes to realisation in the individual life as τέλειος βίος, it is a human possibility devoid of any 'eschatological' character, except that it is only in the Deity that the μακαρία ζωή always achieves realisation, and at the most only occasionally in us, because our nature is not simple, and is therefore subject to change (Aristot. *Eth. Nic.* VII.15, p. 1154b, 21 ff.).

ii. *Hellenistic usage*

(a) *Stoicism*. In Stoicism it is the concept of ζωή drawn from the scientific tradition which predominates. Ζωή, seen as movement in the widest sense,[1] is the physical life that stirs in everything organic. It is however, made quite clear that the actual achievement of life is no mere natural process, that to live according to nature, or agreeably to, or following nature (cf. the index to von Arnim) does not accomplish itself but has to be undertaken and realised with intelligent determination.

(b) *Neo-Platonism*. The tradition of anthropological dualism was used by Plato in the service of an idealist conception of soul and life. Neo-Platonism revived this and combined it with new influences from oriental dualism, without the least intention of abandoning the idealist concept of ζωή. This may be clearly seen in the writings of Plotinus.

(c) *Gnosticism*. Whereas in Plotinus the truly divine life is always described by some epithet like ἀληθινή, in Gnosticism ζωή by itself means the divine life. In the

---

[1] E. Norden, *Agnostos Theos* (1913), pp. 19-22; cf. also von Arnim, II, pp. 285, 26 ff.; 287, 33 ff.

usage of Plotinus, although he is not wholly consistent, the connection with the Greek tradition is clearly preserved, in so far as he distinguishes true life as something specifically human, and therefore consciously undertaken and accomplished in intellectual activity, from mere natural existence. This distinction is abandoned in Gnosticism. 'Life', in the context of Gnostic dualism, lies wholly on the divine side of the dividing-line. This means that 'life' has lost the meaning of a truly human life: it is thought of as a physical phenomenon. It is not regarded, however, as the mere existence of cosmic beings, but as their imperishable permanence, and at the same time as the power on which this is based, which prevails over every obstacle. Ζωή is regarded as something in the process of becoming, which is found in its pure form in the divine world and which emanates from it as a mysterious fluid and can be present in men and things.[1] It is no longer the ψυχή, as the natural life-force, which is regarded as its bearer, but the πνεῦμα, the divine breath of life. In the dualistic outlook of Gnosticism, then, 'life' is regarded as the completely other-worldly divine power, or sometimes as the freedom from corruption that depends on it, so that such ζωή cannot be perceived at all in the earthly life and its phenomenal existence.

From this it is plain that the concept of ζωή means a concept of a true life beyond this world, which ought to have, and, in so far as ζωή includes a distinct understanding of the self and experience, does have the character of being 'my' life in particular. But since man is delivered from his historical separateness in the redemption of the true man from the body which gave him his first experience of the concrete possibilities of life in history, freedom from death becomes in actual fact freedom from the real possibilities of human

[1] cf. TWNT II, pp. 286 ff.

existence. Man's understanding of himself, his knowledge, that is, of his origin and destiny, when guided
by the myth of the Original Man loses any sense of
knowledge of his own particular origin and destiny
and becomes a matter of general speculation. When
ζωή is thought of in a non-temporal way, it can in
practice be thought of only as a state of physical
existence; and, in so far as this ζωή is thought of as
his own ζωή in particular, it can be thought of only as a
physical condition and defined in purely negative
terms: it is essentially in negations that it is realised.[1]

2. Death

i. Classical usage

Although in the old popular Greek view death does
not mean a complete end of human existence, in so
far as the dead man leads a shadowy existence in
Hades, this does not really count as life. What life
really means is ended by death and no one must
underrate the horror of death (Homer, *Od.* 11.487 ff.).
Life is the highest good. Apart from the idea of the
translation of individual heroes to the 'Islands of the
Blest' and the belief current in 'Orphic' and Pythagorean circles that death is a liberation of the soul imprisoned in the body and the doctrine held in these
circles of the transmigration of souls, death counted as

[1] In this sphere *Zωή* can now be hypostatised as a divine figure,
as inscriptions show. That we find in the Valentinian ogdoad the
syzygies of aeons *Λόγος-Zωή* (W. Bousset, *Die Hauptprobleme der
Gnosis* [1907], pp. 163, 340) may be due to John i.4; but it is
only rendered possible by the Gnostic view of ζωή. In the representation of Paradise in a Christian fresco from Egypt the first
human couple are depicted as Adam and Zoe. L. Troje (*ΑΔΑΜ
und ΖΩΗ*) conjectures that this should be interpreted on the basis
of Gnostic mythology, so that Adam = Light. The name Zoe,
given to several Byzantine empresses, has arisen from the use of
ζωή (like κεφαλή) as a term of endearment (cf. Juvenal 6.195).

the end of life and accordingly as a thing of terror.[1]
Why, otherwise, should the blessed gods not die?
(Sappho in Aristot. *Rhet.* II.23, p. 1398b, 27 ff.).
Death may be the universal fate of men (there is an old
proverb 'We must all pay the debt of death'), but that
is no consolation; the inevitability of death casts its
shadow over every life and puts a question-mark
against its whole meaning. There is more consolation
in the knowledge that life itself, with all its toil and
distress, is a doubtful boon, so that it may appear better
never to have been born or, having been born, to die at
once. Death brings peace and suicide can sometimes
appear as a liberation from shame and suffering. And
yet, when death comes, no one wants to die. Finally,
moreover, we do not know what comes after death.

As, however, the Homeric heroes venture their lives
for fame, fame and glory always afford the possibility
of treating death as an achievement, and so making it
part of life. The man who has fallen in glorious strife
enjoys immortal life on earth in the form of continuing
fame, and perhaps the dead hear something of this
fame. On the other hand, the heroic courage which
embraces death is not necessarily accompanied by
reflection on glory: 'I would not accept life at the price
of being a coward' (Plat. *Alc.* 115d). Above all, death
for one's πόλις, in which renown lives on, is something

---

[1] Unlike ζωή, θάνατος was personified and given artistic representation. True, Lessing's picture of ὕπνος and θάνατος as
brothers (cf. Hom. *Il.*16.671 ff. and 14.231; Hes. *Theog.* 211 f.,
756 ff.) in *How the Ancients represented Death* is not typical of popular
belief. In the famous lecythus painting ὕπνος is probably delivering
the dead man to the daemon of the grave. The conception of
death as a dreadful daemon in the *Alcestis* of Euripides is characteristic of the popular notion. The actual figure of Death is rare,
but we must seek its representation in art particularly in pictures
of monsters of the ghostly underworld, and these are found in
Etruscan vase paintings also.

fine. In this way to die nobly becomes the characteristic Greek form of victory over death.

It thus becomes plain that Greek thought did not originally regard death as a natural phenomenon, but as the destiny of specifically human existence, with which each man must come to terms for himself. It is, however, equally characteristic of Greek thought to try to come to terms with death by interpreting it as a natural phenomenon.

The problem of death is treated by Euripides and Plato in a way that is characteristic of the Greek outlook. The positive answer is given in the Platonic philosophy. In the *Apology* it is expressly denied that death and life have value as such, or that man can know whether death is a good or an evil (29a). The problem of death is lifted on to a different plane: in place of the question of good or evil we must put that of right or wrong (28b, 29b), and man must answer this question, which applies to all his actions. It is not being dead but dying that concerns him: it becomes an achievement; for the situation of dying gives a man once more the opportunity to prove himself good or bad, and so undergo the final test of obedience that God requires (28d, 38e ff., 41d ff.). The *Phaedo* goes further still. It develops the proposition that the truly philosophical attitude to life is that it is a preparation for death (64a, 67e, 80e). This enables us to see in what sense death can be the test of life. It is not in the necessity of accepting it as the unintelligible destiny which comes at the end of a just life, but positively, in the sense that the just life finds its fulfilment in the death for which it has always been striving to prepare. For death affects the body alone, whereas the life of the philosopher consists precisely in the liberation of the soul from the body. Plato may be here following the 'Orphic' and Pythagorean tradition in his imagery, but his real meaning is not dualistic as that tradition is, for philosophic purification is no mere asceticism, but a positive attitude to life. The importance of this tradition lies, therefore, in the fact that it has become the vehicle for the transmission of the idea that the real life of man is not just a natural phenomenon. It is in the strife against lusts and pleasures in the service of virtue or wisdom that this reality is achieved (82c, 107c, d, 114c). True ζωή is not given but given up; whereas death as a natural process belongs to the sphere of the given. If, then, true life is a liberation of the soul from the body, the philosopher cannot be afraid of the end of bodily existence in death. That the soul will continue to exist he cannot know, but there is a 'great hope' (114c, d). This hope—and along with it, the attempts that have been made to 'prove' immortality—is not the basis of the philosophical attitude to death but arises out of it. Belief in immortality is therefore a venture (κίνδυνος, 114d); what is an absolute obligation is to accept the claim of virtue, and this forbids us to look upon the soul as a bodily object, or upon life as a natural process and therefore on death as a mere natural phenomenon.

In the period which follows, all these motifs are still at work. Aristotle's analysis of ζωή as a natural phenomenon means that for him death too can be only a natural phenomenon; it is the extinction of the ψυχή, the life force of the bodily organism. As it can exist only when the two are united, it must have its end at death. True, the νοῦς, which has come into the ψυχή from outside, is immortal, but at death it is detached from body and soul and we are completely in the dark about the manner of its continued existence. This does not, however, prevent Aristotle from regarding death as an achievement.

ii. *Hellenistic usage*

(a) Stoicism. In Stoicism death is expressly understood as a natural phenomenon, though in the same inconsistent way as ζωή.[1] (cf. p. 25) We cannot quite say that in Epictetus and Marcus Aurelius the present moment in which life has to achieve reality is dissolved into timelessness. It is, however, characteristic that the present is never understood as bound up with the past, and with a man's own past in particular. Because man is not seen as bound together by guilt or sin, he appears free in relation to death; he can be master of his own fears, because death need never acquire the character of a judgement upon him.

It is not therefore death which threatens the reality of life but the corruption which consists in adopting an unphilosophical attitude to life, in giving up the pursuit of virtue and devoting oneself to external life and its good things. Since this is what constitutes the threat to true life, it can be described as death or dying, and the body and external goods are called dead. Indeed, men who have not been awakened to the philosophic life and their whole circumstances are described as dead (νεκρός).

(b) Neo-Platonism. The usage here also belongs to Hellenistic dualism. For Plotinus it is death for the soul 'while still sunk in body to lie down in matter and drench itself with it', i.e. to sink in wickedness (*Enn.* I. viii.13, p. 112, 15 ff.). Plotinus is not, of course, a thorough-going dualist, since he ascribes positive functions to the soul which is bound to the body; only for the bad man is this earthly ζωή altogether an evil. The bodily ζωή, however, is at best only a shadow (ἴχνος) of the true life, and the body is a chain or tomb of the soul. The freer it becomes from the body, the

---

[1] E. Benz, *Das Todesproblem in der stoischen Philosophie* (1929).

more it achieves true life. For this reason bodily death, which is objective liberation from body and soul, is no evil but a good, for it is the consummation (as it was for Plato) of the end for which the soul is striving. Nevertheless suicide is repudiated as an unwarranted taking of the law into our own hands.

(c) Gnosticism. In the dualistic sections of the *Corpus Hermeticum* a much more radical view is taken of bodily life as true death, in which true ζωή cannot develop. The death of the body is therefore liberation, as in Gnosticism generally. Here, however, true ζωή is not understood in a philosophical sense, but is simply the immortality of the divine life. Accordingly the transition to this is here seen as an organic transition only in so far as earthly life has been put to death by asceticism. Furthermore, immortality or incorruption, as in the Mystery Religions (and these are largely the basis of Gnosticism), are assured by means of sacraments, or rather through ecstatic mystical experiences in which the original sacraments have been spiritualised. When the soul lays aside the body in the mystery of rebirth or in the journey to heaven, it attains to ζωή.

III. EVIDENCE FROM THE SEPTUAGINT AND JUDAISM

1. Ζωή and βίος in the Septuagint

In the LXX the words ζῆν and ζωή almost exactly coincide with the Hebrew original *ḥyh* and *ḥayyīm*. The noun *ḥayyīm* occurs 147 times in the Masoretic text; in addition there are also two passages in Daniel with *ḥayyīm*. Of these 149 instances the LXX has translated 130 by ζωή and 10 by ζῆν. Of the remaining 9 instances 3 are not found in the LXX, so that only on 6 occasions is there a different and, for the most part, free rendering. Βίος occurs only once for *yᵉmē ḥayyīm* in Prov. xxxi.12. In this passage ΑΣΘ have the literal ἡμέραι τῆς ζωῆς. At all events the LXX has maintained in translation the old distinction between ζωή as the *vita qua vivimus* and βίος as the *vita quam vivimus*,[1] at least in so far as βίος 11 times in Job and twice in Proverbs (iii.2, 16) renders *yāmīm* in the sense of duration of life, whilst ζωή, even in these books as in the rest of the OT, is reserved for *ḥayyīm*.[2] Βίος incidentally does not occur at all in the Law and the Prophets. Even in the Hellenistic part of the OT (Wisdom, II and III Maccabees) βίος is mostly the length of life. Only in IV Maccabees, in the ὀρθός or νόμιμος βίος does the ethical character obtrude.

Ζωή occurs 278 times in the LXX, of which 191 are in the books of the Hebrew canon. On 141 occasions it is

---

[1] R. C. Trench, *Synonyms of the N.T.* (1876), pp. 88 ff.

[2] But cf. Ecclus. xl.29. Prov. iv.10c is a parallel translation of 10b. The verb βιοῦν only appears 5 times as a translation, besides twice in Wisdom and twice in IV Macc. without a Masoretic original. Three times it renders *ḥyh* (Prov. vii.2; ΑΣΘ ζῆν; ix.6 [only A, א²; B has βασιλεύειν; ΑΣΘ, ζῆν]; Ecclus. xl.28). *yāmīm* is only in Job vii.1b translated by ζωή, probably with the purpose of a change of expression from βίος, used by the LXX in verse 1a.

the translation of *ḥayyīm*[1] and on 21 occasions it corresponds to a form of *ḥyh*. In the remaining 29 instances the LXX adds the word of its own accord 10 times without a Masoretic basis and in 19 cases it is a question of a free rendering of the Hebrew or of misunderstandings or mistakes on the part of the copyist or translator.

The concept of life only really becomes a moral and religious term in the hagiographa and the Apocrypha.[2] Corresponding to the Hebrew *ḥayyīm*, ζωή always retained the purely quantitative meaning in the Greek Bible, yet in many passages the sense of the Greek ζωή unwittingly gives rise to a valuation of life which goes beyond the old Israelite idea of long life. In the LXX ζωή and ζῆν, as translations of the stem *ḥyh* signify first and foremost duration and strength of life in contrast with death and illness. Thus σὰρξ ζῶσα (Gen. viii.21; Lev. xiii.10) and ψυχὴ ζῶσα (Gen. ii.7, 19 *et al*. ΑΣ also Gen. 1.30 LXX, ψυχὴ ζωῆς) are mentioned side by side. All creatures are bearers of ψυχὴ ζωῆς (Gen. 1.30; Σ I Sam. 1.26, cf. II Sam. xv.21), πνοὴ ζωῆς (Gen. ii.7, vii.22),[3] πνεῦμα ζωῆς (Gen. vi.17, vii.15; Judith x.13) without its being possible to distinguish clearly between these various expressions in practice.[4] But because this animal vitality is a gift from God, ζωή attains its special meaning as a concept of value. Where in Deut. xxxii.39 it says ἐγὼ ἀποκτεννῶ καὶ ζῆν ποιήσω (cf. Dan. iv.34a), God is thereby represented as the Lord

---

[1] The figure of 130 given above, is based on the 147 references to *ḥayyīm* given by Mandelkern. The other 11 references are given by Mandelkern under *ḥay*.

[2] ζωή appears in the historical books 54 times, in the prophets 43 times but 94 times in the hagiographa, including Daniel, and 87 times in the Apocrypha.

[3] cf. also ἐμπνέον ζωῆς, Josh. x.40.

[4] Philo, *Leg. All.* III.161 and *Det. Pot. Ins.* 80 give πνεῦμα for πνοή in Gen. ii.7.

over life and death following the same pattern as the belief in him as creator; he is the Lord of history who strikes his people but who heals them again. That at least is the original sense of the text. In late Judaism, however, the divine gift of life, which is here mentioned primarily in the natural sense, has been understood in the sense of the eschatological religion of salvation as the saving gift of eternal life. Thus IV Macc. xviii.18, together with Ezek. xxxvii and Prov. iii.18 (ξύλον ζωῆς), is quoted as a proof of resurrection and eternal life. In this, it is connected quite simply with the traditional wishful idea of long life, as IV Maccabees makes plain: xvii.12 ἀφθαρσία ἐν ζωῇ πολυχρονίῳ and xviii.19 αὕτη ἡ ζωὴ ὑμῶν καὶ ἡ μακρότης (א) τῶν ἡμερῶν, which significantly becomes changed to μακρίοτης in A. Cf. also xv.3: τὴν εὐσέβειαν . . . τὴν σῴζουσαν εἰς αἰώνιον ζωὴν κατὰ θεόν; xvi.25: διὰ τὸν θεὸν ἀποθανόντες ζῶσιν τῷ θεῷ (cf. vii.19). This same understanding of Deut. xxxii.39 as found in the Hellenistic IV Maccabees is also expounded in the Rabbinical tradition.[1] Deut. xxxii.39 is quoted here with others and interpreted in the same sense as proof for the resurrection of the dead. Since the time of the Maccabees the belief in a world beyond, in resurrection and eternal life, had received complete and widespread recognition in Jewish theology,[2] even if it had apparently hardly spread among the people both then and up to early Christian times. Thus in the oldest of the preserved Jewish tomb inscriptions, which are particularly important as evidence of the Jewish piety in the Roman period, a

---

[1] cf. Str.-B. I, p. 894, and S. Krauss, *Sanhedrin-Makkot* (1933), p. 267 (Giessner Mishnah, IV.4-5).

[2] cf. Dan. xii.2 LXX θ: ζωή αἰώνιος for ḥayyē 'ōlām; II Macc. vii.9; εἰς αἰώνιον ἀναβιώσιν ζωῆς; vii.14: ἀνάστασις εἰς ζωὴν; vii.23: τὸ πνεῦμα καὶ τὴν ζωὴν ὑμῖν πάλιν ἀποδίδωσιν μετ'ἐλέους; vii.36: πόνον ἀενάου ζωῆς.

belief in the world beyond is only quite seldom implied. Where βιοῦν and ζῆν occur in tomb inscriptions the words refer to the duration and the kind of earthly life lived.[1] Despite this, however, in tomb inscriptions there is occasionally to be found a quotation from the OT used as evidence of the belief in the world beyond. The metaphor used by Abigail (I Sam. xxv.29) of the *bundle of life* ṣᵉrōr haḥayyîm δεσμὸς τῆς ζωῆς, has since the Middle Ages become more and more the confession of Judaism at the graveside.[2] These words, it is true, are first found on a Hebrew inscription in the Christian cemetery of Antinoe in Egypt in the second century, but may be cited without hesitation in support of the developing belief in the resurrection, even that of the Judaism of the early Christian era, and in support of the popular Jewish understanding of the text at the time, especially as the same word has also been used in a similar context by the Rabbis. They intend this to prove the sojourn of the souls of the righteous in the immediate presence of God (B. Hag. 12b).[3] In doing this Judaism probably understood the δεσμὸς τῆς ζωῆς somehow as a φάρμακον ζωῆς (Ecclus. vi.16: ṣᵉrōr

---

[1] The inscriptions show no obvious linguistic distinction in expressing the ideas; but βιοῦν in the formula καλῶς βιώσας and similar expressions signifies more often the ethical character of a life. Cf. e.g. N. Müller-N. A. Bees, *Der Inschriften der jüd. Katakombe am Monteverde zu Rom* (1919), Nos. 30, 34 (on the other hand καλῶς ἔζησεν Nos. 66, 112), and H. W. Beyer-H. Lietzmann, *Die jüd. Katakombe der Villa Torlonia in Rom* (1930), inscriptions Nos. 6, 25, 42. διὰ βίου in these inscriptions means 'lifelong' (Müller-Bees, Nos. 109, 175). ζῆν is mostly used for stating the age of a person: ἔζησεν ἐτῶν . . . (many examples).

[2] Moreover the letters tnṣbh are used as an abbreviation for the phrase (in Hebrew): 'May his life be bound up in the bundle of life.' Cf. G. Bertram, 'The Problem of death in popular Judaeohellenistic piety' *Crozer Quarterly* 10 (1938), p. 286. [Cf. O. Eissfeldt, *Der Beutel der Lebendigen* (1960), p. 32.]

[3] Str.-B. III, p. 532.

haḥayyīm).¹ Such a φάρμακον, that is an agent that mysteriously produces life, is obviously present in the ξύλον ζωῆς (Gen. iii.22 ff.; Isa. lxv.22; Prov. iii.18; IV Macc. xviii.16). Even the ξύλον δι᾽οὗ γίνεται δικαιοσύνη (Wisd. xiv.7) belongs in our context for it is the means, φάρμακον, of the preservation of life for the world. Thus δικαιοσύνη corresponds here to life as the blessing of salvation. And so the word ζωή is used occasionally where in the Masoretic text this blessing is described in some other way. For example, in Hos. x.12 ζωή is used for *ḥesed*: σπείρατε ἑαυτοῖς εἰς δικαιοσύνην, τρυγήσατε (reap) εἰς καρπὸν ζωῆς, φωτίσατε ἑαυτοῖς φῶς γνώσεως. The ideas of φῶς and γνῶσις were probably also first inserted into the text of the LXX as a result of misunderstanding so that ζωή, φῶς, γνῶσις, here, as so frequently in late Judaism, stand together. Thus the knowledge of life in Prov. xxii.19 is spoken of in ΑΣ thus: γνωστὴν ἐποίησά σοι ζωήν; Masoretic: *hōdaʿtīkā hayyōm ʾap-ʾāttā* which the LXX translates καὶ γνωρίσῃ σοι τὴν ὁδόν σου. The formulation φῶς ζωῆς has found its way into a sentence, in itself easily understandable but one which no longer satisfies the particular religious need. Prov. xvi.15 *bᵉʾōr-pᵉnē-melek-ḥayyīm;* this is correctly translated by ΑΣΘΕ′ as ἐν φωτὶ προσώπου βασιλέως ζωή, while the LXX substitutes ἐν φωτὶ ζωῆς υἱὸς βασιλέως. *ʾōr haḥayyīm* and *ʾereṣ ḥayyīm* are obviously normal descriptions of that human sphere of life which can easily be rendered literally in Greek. This is also the case with Ps. lvi [LXX lv]. 13 [Heb. and LXX 14] where the Masoretic text *lᵉhithallēk lipnē ʾelōhīm bᵉʾōr*, so far as it is important for us here, is translated literally by the LXX: τοῦ εὐαρεστῆσαι ἐνώπιον τοῦ θεοῦ ἐν φωτὶ ζώντων. Σ on the other hand has ὥστε ὁδεύειν ἔμπροσθεν τοῦ θεοῦ διὰ

---

¹ A. Marmorstein, ZAW NF 2(1925), pp. 119-124.

φωτὸς τῆς ζωῆς, so that φῶς τῆς ζωῆς must appear as the gift of grace through which life before God is possible. In Isa. liii.8 Σ as well as Θ translate *mē'ereṣ ḥayyîm* with ἐκ (ἀπὸ) γῆς ζώντων while the LXX on the other hand separates the concepts of γῆ and ζωή and thus arrives at the sentence αἴρεται ἀπὸ τῆς γῆς ἡ ζωή αὐτοῦ which points to the liberation from the earth of the life of the Servant of God.[1] *'ōr haḥayyîm* in the sense used above stands also in Job xxxiii.30 in the Masoretic text and Θ translates it correspondingly τοῦ ἐπιστρέψαι ψυχὴν αὐτοῦ ἐκ διαφθορᾶς, τοῦ φωτίσαι αὐτῳ ἐν φωτὶ ζώντων, giving a strictly 'this worldly' orientation. Here again, however, the LXX, by its choice of expression, makes it possible to interpret the sentence in terms of the belief in the world beyond. Indeed the translation itself perhaps presupposes such an understanding: ἀλλ' ἐρύσατο τὴν ψυχήν μου ἐκ θανάτου, ἵνα ἡ ζωή (A א² ψυχή) μου ἐν φωτί αἴνῃ αὐτόν. This corresponds to the statement of xxxiii.28: ἡ ζωή (א² ψυχή) μου φῶς ὄψεται. Also Job xi.17 where the LXX apart from σοι agrees with the Masoretic text, is probably to be understood in this way: ἐκ δὲ μεσημβρίας ἀνατελεῖ σοι ζωή.[2]

The fact that 'Life' in the LXX is conceived essentially in the sense of eternal life is most clearly seen from the LXX translation of the famous passage in Job xix.25 where the LXX renders the Hebrew word *ḥay*,

---

[1] K. F. Euler, *Die Verkündigung vom leidenden Gottesknecht aus Js. 53 in der griech. Bibel* (BWANT IV, 1934), pp. 26, 71, 128 f. The LXX formulation perhaps refers to the Assumption of Isaiah.

[2] ζωή for *ḥeled: ḥeled* Ps. xxxix [LXX xxxviii].5 [Heb.+LXX 6], lxxxix [LXX lxxxviii].47 [Heb. +LXX 48]is rendered ὑπόστασις, living creature; differently Judg. vi.4: *miḥyā* is rendered ὑπόστασις ζωῆς, livelihood. Otherwise *ḥeled* only appears in Ps. xvii [LXX xvi]. 14 (γῆ) and Ps. xlix. [LXX xlviii]. 1[Heb.+LXX 2] (οἰκουμένη). For the designation of the south as the side of life, cf. Lact. *Inst.* II.9, CSEL 19.143, lines 19-21; in addition F. J. Dolger, *Die Sonne der Gerechtigkeit und der Schwarze* (1919), p. 44.

living, by ἀέναος, eternal: gō'ᵃlī ḥāy wᵉ'aḥᵃrōn 'al 'āpār
yāqūm: ἀέναος ἐστιν ὁ ἐκλύειν με μέλλων ἐπὶ γῆς.[1] Θ
translates it more literally: ὁ ἀγχιστεύς (next of kin)
μου ζῇ καὶ ἔσχατον ἐπὶ χώματος ἀναστήσει. An interpretation of the text in the sense of an eschatological
gift of salvation is also given to Prov. ix.6 by using
εἰς τὸν αἰῶνα βασιλεύσητε, which ΑΣΘ render by
ζήσεσθε.

Moreover the resurrection passages in the Masoretic
text should be regarded to a certain extent as starting
points for the understanding of ζωή in the Greek
Bible. (In addition to those mentioned above, in the
present context Isa. xxvi.19 should be referred to

---

[1] The treatment of the passage by F. X. Wutz, Die Transkrip-
tionen von der LXX bis zu Hieronymus (1933), p. 331 does not do
justice to the peculiarity of the LXX. Cf. the rendering of ḥay
by θνητός, where it is used of man as mortal; Job xxx.23: οἰκία γὰρ
παντὶ θνητῷ γῆ. In corresponding cases the translation of the root
ḥyḥ with ζωή or ζῆν is usually avoided and there are inserted,
for example, ἄνθρωπος, ψυχή (on the other hand Job vii.15 A
ζωή renders nepeš), ζῷον, θήρ, θηρίον, etc. Perhaps in Ezek.
xxxii.23, 24, 26, 32 the replacement of γῆς by τῆς, in various MSS.,
has happened instinctively because the connection of γῆ and true
ζωή seemed to be impossible. Nevertheless ζωή is also used in the
devaluated sense of earthly life; Eccles. ix.9: ζωὴ ματαιότητος;
Wisd. i.12: πλάνη ζωῆς; xii.23: ἀφροσύνη ζωῆς; xv.12: ζωή-
παίγνιον. Also Ps. lvi.8 [Heb. 9 LXX lv.9] where the hapaxlego-
menon nōd, ephemeral life, is translated ζωή, where ζωή seems to
imply the meanness and pitiableness of life. More often ζωή is used
in the sense of sustenance, so Prov. v.9 for hōd; xxiii.3, xxvii.27 for
leḥem. But in the latter verse the LXX has obviously made a
deliberate alteration in the interests of a deepening of religious
meaning. While the Masoretic text talks of goat's milk as food,
LXX understands the verse as the end of the warning and
refers εἰς ζωήν to the acceptance of the warning: υἱέ, παρ' ἐμοῦ
ἔχεις ῥήσεις ἰσχυρὰς εἰς τὴν ζωήν σου καὶ εἰς τὴν ζωήν τῶν (ℵ) σῶν
θεραπόντων. Here also the attempt of Wutz, op. cit. pp. 244 f.,
to explain the LXX version philologically simply by means of
an hypothesis of transcription appears misguided.

particularly: *yiḥyū mētēkā*, which the LXX renders ἀναστήσονται; ᾿ΑΣΘ on the other hand ζήσονται.) Even where the translator did not yet have first and foremost the transcendental gift of salvation in his mind, the reader or hearer was bound, as a result of his belief, to replace a purely worldly understanding by the eschatological interpretation in which the faith and life of the godly man could appear as a precondition or even as the anticipation of eternal life. This is the sense in which the circles which believed in the resurrection would have understood the corresponding promises of the OT Law and the Prophets: Lev. xviii.5; Amos. v.4, 14; Isa. lv.3; Ezek. xviii.32(A), etc. On this basis the metaphors of the OT Wisdom literature are intelligible: ὁδός ζωῆς Ps. xvi [LXX xv]. 11; Prov. iv.23 (ἔξοδαι); v.6, vi.23; viii.35,[1] x.17, xv.24, xvi.17; cf. Jer. xxi.8; φῶς ζωῆς Ps. lvi.13 [Heb. 14; LXX lv.14] Σ; δένδρον ζῶης Prov. xi.30 (᾿ΑΣΘ: ξύλον ζωῆς, cf. also remarks above); xiii.12, xv.4; πηγή ζωῆς Prov. xiii.14, xiv.27, xvi.22, xviii.4 (Mas. ḥokmā, ᾿ΑΣΘ σοφίας); Ecclus. xxi.13, cf. Jer. ii.13, xvii.13 and further Bar. iii.9: ἐντολὰς ζωῆς; Ezek. xxxiii.15: πρόσταγμα ζωῆς. The wisdom literature conveys the idea of life not only in the sense of happiness or length of natural life but as salvation which points beyond the earthly sphere, life, therefore, in the eschatological and at the same time mystic (gnostic) sense. This must also be assumed in numerous passages in the Psalms. In Ps. cxix [LXX cxviii] there is, for example, the frequently recurring ζῆσόν με. In Ps. xlix.9 [LXX xlviii.10], it can be seen how the idea of eternal life is expressed in the Greek translations in a new and unambiguous form although in contrast with the Masoretic text it was obviously brought

---

[1] The LXX here is independent. The Masoretic text corresponds to the translation of ᾿ΑΣΘ: ὁ γὰρ εὑρών με εὑρήσει ζωήν (wisdom is speaking).

a priori to the text. Ps. xlix.7, 9 [Heb. 8b, 10] according to the Masoretic text reads: *nor give to God a ransom for him, that he should live alway, that he should not see the pit.*[1] The LXX renders the passage (xlix.9 [LXX xlviii.10]) καὶ ζήσεται εἰς τέλος ὅτι οὐκ ὄψεται καταφθοράν. Ἀ reads καὶ ἐπαύσατο εἰς αἰῶνα καὶ ζήσεται εἰς νῖκος. Σ expresses most clearly the belief in resurrection and eternal life: ἀλλὰ παυσάμενος τῷ αἰῶνι τούτῳ, ζῶν εἰς αἰῶνα διατελέσει.

2. Palestinian Judaism

(a) *Life and Death*. In Palestinian Judaism the OT idea of life is retained throughout.[2] Human beings, who above all are the subjects of life, can be described simply as the living ones.[3] Life is the extent in time of natural existence; *days of life* often means *life*.[4] It goes without saying that life depends on food (Ecclus. xxix.21, xxxix.26, etc.) and likewise that God is lord over death and life (Ecclus. xi.14; Wisd. xvi.13; IV Macc. xviii.18). He is invoked as *father and God of my*

---

[1] So F. Baethgen (²1897). The emendations of A. Bertholet in Kautzsch (*ad. loc.*) can hardly be thought to restore the original text. H. Gunkel in his translation uses a hypothetical sentence and thus preserves the negative sense of the passage.

[2] Not all sources can be clearly assigned to Palestinian or Hellenistic Judaism. In the Greek Ecclesiasticus, in Wisdom and the Test. XII Patr. and others, Palestinian and Hellenistic motifs are mixed so that these texts are used in this and the following section.

[3] Tob. xii.6; Ecclus. vii.33, etc., cf. Dan. ii.30, LXX: τοὺς ἀνθρώπους; Θ: τοὺς ζῶντας following the Aramaic ḥayyayyā'.

[4] e.g. Tob. i.3, iv.3; Judith x.3, xvi.22; Ecclus. (Heb.) iii.12; often in Test. XII Patr. (*My*) *days* = (*my*) *life*, e.g. Test. Iss. vii.5; Zeb. i.4; Dan i.1. Ecclus. l.1 (Gk.) ζωή and ἡμέραι in parallel, (Heb.) *dōr* and *yāmīm*. Cf. also Ecclus. xxxvii.25 (Heb.): *The life of a man lasts for days which may be counted, but the life of Jeshurun for days which cannot be counted.*

life (Ecclus. xxiii.1, 4). He bestows life.[1] He has put the spirit of life in man.[2] He is the *living* God.[3]

Life is a treasure (Ecclus. xxxiv.17; Tobit viii.17, xii.9 ff.; Bar. iii.14). As life is desired for another in greeting him [4] so also *to live* means *to be* or *become well, to be saved*.[5] Long life is the reward for good conduct, evil living shortens life.[6] But death is better than a wretched life.[7] So long as the presupposition remains that with death everything is at an end,[8] this idea serves as a warning to use life wisely. God's commandments

---

[1] II Macc. vii.22 f., xiv.46; Schlatter, *Johannes*, p. 173 on vi.33.

[2] Tg. J. I. on Gen. ii.7 (ZNW 12 (1911), pp. 229 f.), Ex. r. 5 on v.2 (Str.-B. III, p. 44), Tanch. *wyḥy* 6 (ed. S. Buber (1885), p. 214). T. Git. 2. 4. The spirit of God as giving strength: Judith xvi.14; Syr. Bar. xxi.4; Str.-B., I, p. 48, III, p. 240. God's work *lives and lasts for ever* Ecclus. xlii.23.

[3] Ex. r. 5 on v.24, Lev. r. 6 on v.1 (Str.-B. III, pp. 44, 54), Schlatter, *Matthäus*, p. 504 on xvi.16. God as the one who *lives for ever* Str.-B. II, p. 674, III, p. 790 (cf. TWNT I, pp. 197 ff.). Transferred to the King, Judith ii.12 (ζῶν ἐγώ); cf. xi.7, xii.4.

[4] Dan. ii.4, iii.9, etc.

[5] Ecclus. xxxi.14; Dan. vi.20 f.; Judith vii.27, xi.3; I Macc. ii.33; Bar. v.5 (Schlatter, *Matthäus*, p. 317 on ix.18). Death is numbered with other evils; Ecclus. xxxix.29, xl.9; Ps. Sol. xiii.2, xv.8. *Grief unto death* as the greatest degree of affliction; Ecclus. xxxvii.2; Ps. Sol. xvi.2; Test. Jos. iii.9 (Illness ἕως θανάτου Test. Reub. i.8).

[6] Ecclus. iv.12; xxxvii.17 f.; Meg. 27b; Taan. 20b; Men. 44a (Str.-B. II, p. 629 on Acts ix.13; IV, pp. 267, 275); Ber. 55a (Str.-B. IV, p. 629).

[7] Ecclus. xxix.24, xxx.17, xl.28 f. (as to the life of the beggar, *his life cannot be recognised as life;* the LXX differentiates: οὐκ ἔστιν αὐτοῦ ὁ βίος ἐν λογισμῷ ζωῆς. On this, cf. R. Smend, *Die Weisheit des Jesus Sir.* (1906), p. 380 *ad loc.*); Tob. iii.6, 15; I Macc. iv.35; II Macc. vi.19; Besah 32b. (Str.-B. I, pp. 566, 819 on Matt. x.10, xix.22): *The life of three is no life* ... In one place suicide is considered as a possibility, Tob. iii.10.

[8] Ecclus. x.11, xvii.27 f. (the dead do not praise God); xxii.11 (the light goes out for the dead). At the same time the old Sheol belief remains.

are commandments of life;[1] his words are words of life;[2] the Torah is the tree of life, the medicine of life.[3] The image of the path of life and of death is often used.[4]

Death is the universal fate of man.[5] The day of death is concealed [6] but death does not tarry [7] so it is always a question of *memento mori*.[8] The fear of death hangs over every man.[9] Even if death is considered as rest,[10] or even, bitter as it is, is sometimes desired,[11] the conviction that it is a punishment for sin nevertheless becomes more and more prevalent.[12] It came into the

[1] Bar. iii.9: ἐντολαὶ ζωῆς; cf. iv.1.

[2] At Sinai God has spoken *words of life* Ex. r. xxix on xx.2 (Str.-B. I, p. 464 and Schlatter, *Johannes*, p. 183 on vi.68; cf. *ibid*. p. 182 on vi.63). Further Str.-B. II, p. 681 on Acts vii.38; III, p. 129 on Rom. iii.1 f.

[3] Str.-B. III, p. 498 on II Cor. ii.16. For the understanding of the *tree of life* as the Torah: Str.-B. II, p. 483 on John vi.35; III.792 on Rev. ii.7; also the *water of life* Str.-B. II, pp. 435, 483, 752.

[4] Men have the choice between life and death, Ecclus. xv.17; xxxiii.14, xxxvii.18. The concept of the two ways: Dalman, WJ I, pp. 130 f., Str.-B. I, pp. 460-463, Bousset-Gressmann, p. 276. In all these cases it is not possible to decide whether it meant life in the old sense, the long and happy life on earth, or in the sense of eternal life which will be discussed later.

[5] Ecclus. xiv.17, xli.3 f. Str.-B. I, pp. 754, 815. For the discussions, whether there are exceptions, and if so, what they are (Enoch, Elijah, etc.): Str.-B. I, pp. 753 f.; III, pp. 744 f.; IV, p. 766. Phrases are used about dying such as to 'see' (Judith vii.27) or 'taste' death (Str.-B. I, pp. 751 f.).

[6] Ecclus. xi.19, xiv.12; Str.-B. II, pp. 126, 412; III, p. 473.

[7] Ecclus. xiv.12.

[8] Ecclus. xxviii.6; Shab. 153a (Str.-B. I, p. 878).

[9] Ecclus. xl.5.   [10] Wisd. iv.7.

[11] Ecclus. xxii.11, xli.1 f. It is easy for a father to die if he has a good son, Ecclus. xxx.4 f.

[12] Str.-B. I, p. 815; III, pp. 155-157, 228 f. Bousset-Gressmann, pp. 399 ff. For discussions on why the righteous must die as well: Str.-B. I, pp. 815 f.; III, pp. 228 f.

world through Adam, or Eve.[1] All human beings have become sinners and guilty of death.[2] This idea, however, can also take the form of saying that death does not come from God but was brought into the world through the devil.[3] The angel of death appears as a diabolical figure.[4]

(b) *Life after death.* The more the life of the individual is at stake, the more oppressive death becomes since it destroys the individual's life. The stronger also becomes the consciousness that life as an individual matter needs continuity to fulfil its essential nature. Death is not part of life but its contradiction. Real life would have to be eternal life. This is the way it must be understood if, as far as can be ascertained, the expectation of an (eternal) life after death gains more and more ground after the time of the Maccabees, a life which has its basis not in the innate power of the soul [5] but rather is created by God through the resurrection from the dead.[6] It is the *ḥayyē 'ōlām* (LXX ζωή αἰώνιος) (first in

[1] Sin and death go back to Eve, Ecclus. xxv.24; Str.-B. I, pp. 137 f.; III, p. 646. Cf. Vit. Ad. Through Adam sin and death came into the world, II Esdr. iii.7, 21 f., vii.118. Syr. Bar. xvii.3; xxiii.4, etc. Str.-B. I, pp. 815 f.; III, pp. 227 f. Bousset-Gressmann, pp. 406 ff. Lietzmann, *Römer* on Rom. v.12.

[2] II Esdr. vii.21 ff., 46, 68; viii.31, 35; Syr. Bar. liv.15 ff.; Str.-B. III, pp. 155-157, 228 f. (cf. *Sin* (1951) in the series.) For the discussion, whether there is death without sin: Str.-B. I, pp. 815 f. ἁμαρτία εἰς θάνατον Test. Iss. vii.1 (variant reading).

[3] Wisd. i.13; ii.24; *Vit. Ad.*, Bousset-Gressmann, pp. 408 f. (cf. TWNT VII, pp. 151-165 and next note).

[4] Str.-B. I, pp. 144-149, 596.

[5] The thought of the immortality of the soul is taken up in Hellenistic Judaism (cf. p. 51).

[6] cf. TWNT I, pp. 368 ff. God makes the dead to live and is praised for this in prayers: Dalman, WJ. I, p. 128; Schlatter, *Johannes*, p. 148 on v.21 (the spirit quickens; *ibid.* p. 181 on vi.63). That is why the dead, because of the resurrection, can be described as living in the sight of God: Str.-B. I, p. 892, cf. IV Macc. vii.19, xvi.25. Death, and the angel of death, will be

Dan. xii.2) to which eternal damnation is the opposite.[1]
Ideas vary as to whether all mankind or only the righteous are raised; whether resurrection takes place in
various stages and also as to how resurrection life is to
be conceived.[2] The belief is sometimes parallel to and
sometimes combined with the older expectations of an
age of salvation. It became a point of academic discussion and is expounded by the Pharisees against the
Sadducees.[3] It is always taken as a matter of course
in apocalyptic writings.[4]

destroyed: Str.-B. III, pp. 481-483; IV, pp. 887 f. In connection
with the hope of resurrection the Sheol conception also changes.
    [1] The terminology differs. Besides *ḥayyē 'ōlām* (contrast *ḥayyē
šā'āh*) translated ζωὴ αἰώνιος there stands *ḥayyē 'ōlām habbā'*
(contrast *ḥayyē 'ōlām hazzeh*), and instead of the latter it can
simply be written *'ōlām habbā'*: Str.-B. I, pp. 808 f, 829; II, pp.
726 f. Dalman, W.J. I, pp. 127-129. Schlatter, *Johannes*, pp. 158 f.
But it can also simply be *ḥayyīm* (ζωή): Str.-B. I, pp. 464, 808 f.,
829. Dalman, WJ I, pp. 129-131, especially in phrases as 'inherit
life', 'gain', 'enter into life'. Str.-B. I, pp. 464, 808 f., 829.
Dalman, WJ I, pp. 129, 131. Bousset-Gressmann, pp. 275 f.
Also the simple verbal phrase 'the dead shall live' is found:
Schlatter, *Johannes*, p. 151. In all the references given on p. 42, n. 8,
43 nn. 1-4, life can also be eschatological life, which is true also of the
phrase 'the Book of Life' where those who are destined for eternal
life are listed; Str.-B. II, pp. 169 f. (*ibid.* pp. 170-176 concerning
the different myths of the heavenly books), III, p. 840. Bousset-
Gressmann, p. 258 (cf. TWNT, I, pp. 613 ff.).
    [2] Str.-B. IV, pp. 1166-1198, whether the resurrection is general
or partial. Concerning ideas of the future world, Str.-B. IV,
pp. 799-976. For Sheol, Gehenna and the Garden of Eden,
ibid. pp. 1016-1165, also consult Str.-B. index. Proofs of the
resurrection, Str.-B. I, pp. 893-897; II, pp. 542 f.; IV, pp. 943 f.
Cf. further Schürer, *Geschichte*, II, pp. 638-648. Bousset-Gressmann,
pp. 269-280. Lietzmann on I Cor. xv.37 f., 54; II Cor. v.1.
Where one only thinks of a single resurrection of the righteous,
to leave the rest of the dead in the grave is the 'second death',
but this expression is also used for assigning them to everlasting
damnation, Str.-B. III, pp. 830 f.
    [3] Str.-B. IV, pp. 799-976, Bousset-Gressmann, pp. 286-289.
    [4] Str.-B. I, pp. 885 f., Bousset-Gressmann, pp. 269-274.

The real question, however, is how far the concept of 'life' as such has been modified by a belief in a life after death and whether eschatological life is really life in a new sense. Doubtless this is often not the case, for the idea of life is not altered by being thought of as a life without end. And if eschatological life is seen naturally as a life without suffering and setback[1] it is in this also that the intrinsic nature of earthly life lies for the OT. Yet a modification does appear since in the first place eschatological life is thought of as life without sin.[2] Then there is a further modification, which occurs to a greater or lesser degree, according to how far the future life is imagined as being free from the present limitations and manifestations of life. Thus the Rabbinic dictum is transmitted in Ber. 17a: *In the world to come there is no eating and drinking, no begetting or propagating, no trade and traffic, neither envy nor enmity nor dispute, but the righteous sit there with their crowns on their heads and bathe themselves in the glory of the Shekinah.*[3] If, therefore, in late Judaism also, apart from the Hellenistic strand, any idealistic and dualistic idea of life beyond has remained absent, there are nevertheless suggestions

---

[1] With death all privation (illness, etc.) at some time will disappear, Str.-B. I, pp. 208 f.; III, pp. 253 f., Bousset-Gressmann, p. 276. Here the idea of 'the tree of life' is important (differing from p. 43, n. 3) whose fruit (and scent) will give, in the future, life and health, Str.-B. I, pp. 593 f.; IV, pp. 1123 f., 1152. Bousset-Gressmann, p. 284. Also from the 'water' which will flow in the time of healing (Str.-B. II, p. 436; III, p. 805) miraculous strength will be had, Str.-B. III, pp. 854-857; IV, pp. 934 f., Bousset-Gressmann, p. 284.

[2] The evil inclination, which vanishes at death (Str.-B. IV, pp. 479 f.), will be destroyed by God in the Messianic age (Str.-B. IV, pp. 482 f.). God will be among the blessed, his spirit will be poured out, etc. (Bousset-Gressmann, pp. 279 f.). That corresponds to the idea of judgement which in this sense is still unknown in the OT (cf. TWNT III, pp. 920 ff.),

[3] To be found with other references in Str.-B. I, p. 890.

which could allow the other-worldly character of eschatological life to be taken seriously. For the most part, however, it goes no further than a mythological description of the heavenly manner of existence.[1]

3. Hellenistic Judaism

(a) *The usage of ζωή and βίος.* The verb ζῆν is used in the usual way of natural life, especially in the common expressions: to be (still) living (e.g. Jos. *Ant.* 4.316 *et al.;* Test. XII Patriarchs, etc.), to escape alive (Jos. *Bell.* 6.189 *et al.*), to get well (again) (Jos. *Vit.* 421 *et al.*). It is worth noting that in the LXX ζῆν is also used in the causative sense for the hiph'il of *ḥyh*, for which the LXX, however, also has ζωοποιεῖν at its disposal.[2] A distinction can be made between ζωή and βίος (e.g. Ecclus. xxix.21 f., xl.29) but often the words are used without distinction. ζωή and βίος stand in parallelism in Wisd. xv.12. βίος is the period of life in the Letter of Aristeas 209, 260 (διεξάγειν); Jos. *Ant.* 11.219 (διάγειν); 19.221 (διὰ βίου τοῦ παντός, but compare with δι᾽ ὅλου τοῦ ζῆν Letter of Aristeas 130 *et al.*). Just as ζῆν plus indication of duration can be used (Jos. *Ant.* 9.165) so βιοῦν also (Jos. *Ant.* 1.346 *et al.*). One can speak of βίον ζῆν (IV Macc. vi.18) and of

---

[1] Descriptions of an angel-like existence with mythological features, Str.-B. I, pp. 209-212. Bousset-Gressmann, pp. 276-278. The idea of a 'heavenly garment' plays a special role; Bousset-Gressmann, pp. 277 f., Windisch, II *Korinther*, pp. 164 f. Also the idea of the 'crowns (garlands)' which the blessed wear, Ber. 17a, etc. in Str.-B. I, pp. 210, 890; III, p. 404; IV, p. 1143, which (as an attribute of the gods of the planets) was probably originally a token of a god-like existence, but then the Greek idea of the crown of victory comes in, Asc. Is. ix; Syr. Bar. xv.8; Test. Ben. iv.1 (στεφάνους δόξης) cf. Bousset-Gressmann, p. 278, J. Weiss, *I Korinther*, p. 248, 1; Dibelius, *Jakobusbrief*, pp. 86 f. Dibelius, *Hermas* on s. VIII. 2.2 f.

[2] H. St. J. Thackeray, *Grammar of O. T. Greek* (1909), p. 269.

ζωὴν βιοῦν (Ecclus. xl.28). Indeed just as βίος (Letter of Aristeas 273, Jos. *Ant.* 1.326 *et al.*) so ζωή can also mean livelihood (Ecclus. iv.1, xxxi.25?; Test. Levi ii.12?)[1].

(b) *The understanding of life and death.* The understanding of life is, of course, widely that of OT Judaism but it is frequently modified under Hellenistic influence. God, the living one (II Macc. vii.33, xv.4; III Macc. vi.28) is naturally considered lord over life and death (Wisd. xvi.13, IV Macc. xviii.18). He bestows life, but when, as such a one, he is called χορηγὸς τῆς ζωῆς (Jos. *Bell.* 2.131) it is Hellenistic terminology.[2] And just as in Jos *Ant.* 12.22 it says: *For both they and we worship the same God the framer of all things. We call him rightly Zeus (Ζῆνα), giving him this name because he implants life in all men*, so also in the Letter of Aristeas 16 the Stoic Zeus etymology is used to describe God's creative nature. And as ζωή is connected with σύστασις in the Letter of Aristeas 154, so also according to the Test. Reuben ii.4 the first of the seven πνεύματα given to man at his creation is the πνεῦμα ζωῆς μεθ' ἧς ἡ σύστασις (or κίνησις) κτίζεται. The consequence is that the soul, the bearer of the cosmic life force, is considered immortal (cf. p. 51).

Hellenistic influence is further evident in that ζωή (ζῆν) and βίος (βιοῦν) are also used of the manner in which life is lived. There now appear such phrases as καλῶς ζῆν (Letter of Aristeas 127, Jos. *Bell* 7.341) or καλῶς βιοῦν (Letter of Aristeas 32, 39, Jos. *Vit.* 257); νομίμως βιοῦν (Jos. *Ap.* 2.217); ἀδίκως ζῆν (Wisd.

---

[1] Josephus uses ἀναβιοῦν (*Ant.* 18, 14) and ἀναβιῶσαι (*Ant.* 8.327, 11.9) instead of ἀναζῆν; βιοτεύειν is used in *Ant.* 13.145; in *Ap.* 1.68 for *leading one's life*. βιωτικά and βίωσις are not in Josephus; βιώσιμος is found for *a worthy life*.

[2] cf. the combination of OT (Gen. ii.7) and Stoic terminology in Wisd. xv.11, (ἠγνόησεν) τὸν ἐμπνεύσαντα αὐτῷ ψυχὴν ἐνεργοῦσαν καὶ ἐμφυσήσαντα πνεῦμα ζωτικόν.

xiv.28, cf. xii.23); ἀσώτως ζῆν (Jos. *Ant.* 12.203); κατὰ τοὺς Ἰουδαίων νόμους ζῆν (Jos. *Ant.* 13.318; cf. IV Macc. xi.5); κατὰ τὰ πάτρια ἔθη ζῆν (Jos. *Ant.* 11.339); μετὰ ἀταραξίας ζῆν (IV Macc. viii.26). Questions are asked about βίῳ συμφέρον καὶ καθῆκον (Letter of Aristeas 284); about the βίος νόμιμος (IV Macc. vii.15); mention is made of the κυβερνᾶν and κατορθοῦν of βίος (Letter of Aristeas 147, 251), and of the σώζεσθαι of the βίοι τῶν ἀνθρώπων (Letter of Aristeas 240). In the phrase πρὸς ἀλήθειαν ζῆν τὸν ... βίον (IV Macc. vi.18), there is evidence of the idea that the true nature of life is achieved if it conforms to an other-worldly norm. This has its equivalent in the genuinely Hellenistic idea of the relative worth of life's span (Wisd. iv.8 f.).

This, further, has its equivalent in a modified concept of death. The old line of thought is preserved when death is frequently considered as sleep (ὕπνος αἰώνιος Test. Iss. vii.9, Test. Dan vii.1; ὕπνος καλός Test. Zeb. x.1, Test. Asher viii.1 *et al.*; κοιμᾶσθαι Test. Simeon viii.1; Test. Judah xxvi.4 *et al.*).[1] But things are seen in the Greek way when, according to Jos. *Bell.* 7.341 there is an 'either-or', ζῆν καλῶς ἢ τεθνάναι, which obtains for the ἀνὴρ ἀγαθός. The age of persecution and martyrdom taught them to see death as a deed. The Jew did not have to learn the deed itself from the Greek—loyalty μέχρι θανάτου (III Macc. vii.16; IV Macc. vi.21, 30; vii.8, 16 *et al.*), the choice of the θάνατος τῆς εὐσεβείας (IV Macc. xv.12) instead of transgressing the Law and desecrating the sanctuary and people (IV Macc. ix.1, 4, xvi.24 *et al.*; I Macc. iii.59; III Macc. i.29)—nevertheless the understanding of the deed is determined by Hellenistic ideas.[2] That

---

[1] If ὕπνος is seen as εἰκὼν τοῦ θανάτου (Test. Reuben iii.1) this is doubtless a Greek concept, cf. Jos. *Bell.* 7.349.

[2] The glorification of martyrdom is found first in Hellenistic Judaism, cf. A. Schlatter, *Der Märtyrer in den Anfangen der Kirche*

is already evident in that ἀποθνήσκειν is often characterised by prepositional phrases as a significant deed
(ἀποθνήσκειν ὑπὲρ τῶν νόμων καὶ τῆς πατρίδος II Macc.
viii.21, cf. vii.9; δοῦναι τὰς ψυχας ὑπὰρ διαθήκης πατέρων
ἡμῶν I Macc. ii.50; with a stronger Greek flavour:
ἀποθνήσκειν ὑπὲρ ἀρετῆν IV Macc. i.8; ὑπὲρ τῆς
καλοκἀγαθίας IV Macc. i.10. Further ἀποθνήσκειν διὰ
τὸν νόμον IV Macc. vi.27; διὰ τὸν θεόν xvi.25; διὰ τὴν
εὐσέβιαν ix.6; περὶ τοῦ νόμου xiii.9, cf. II Macc. vii.37;
χάριν τῶν ἀδελφῶν ἡμῶν I Macc. ix.10).¹ Such a death
is called καλός (Jos. Bell 7.337), ἀοίδιμος (glorious)
(IV Macc. x.1), μακάριος (IV Macc. x.15); mention
is made of the ἀνδρείᾳ or εὐγενῶς ἀποθανεῖν (I Macc. ix.10;
II Macc. xiv.42). The death of the martyrs is a
ὑπόδειγμα γενναιότητος καὶ μνημόσυνον ἀρετῆς (II Macc.
vi.31, cf. Jos. Bell 7.351). The great speech of Eleazar in
Jos. Bell 7.341-388 is, in particular, carried along on the
ideas of late Stoicism about life and death;² in the
struggle ὑπὲρ τῆς ἐλευθερίας it is a question of esteeming
death as καλόν (337, 341); it is not death but life that
is a συμφορά; death is a liberation of the soul which has
been bound to the θνητὸν σῶμα and whose life in the
σῶμα is, in reality, a τεθνηκέναι (344-358);³ thus one is not
to fear death, but to have ἑτοιμότης πρὸς θάνατον (350 f.).

(1915), pp. 13 ff.; according to genuine Jewish feeling the days
on which the martyrs died were days of disaster, *ibid.* pp. 61 f.

¹ However, it is a characteristically Jewish thought when the
death of the martyr is thought of as vicarious suffering of punishment, II Macc. vii.37; IV Macc. vi.28 f.; xvii.22 (ἱλαστήριος
θάνατος), cf. O. Schmitz, *Die Opferanschauung des späteren Judentums*
(1910), pp. 99 f., 129-132 (cf. TWNT III, pp. 319 ff.). Ἀποθνήσκειν
ὑπὲρ ὑμῶν ἐν πολέμοις ὁρατοῖς καὶ ἀοράτοις is unclear, said of Levi
in Test. Reuben vi.12. Test. Ben. iii.8: ὁ ἀναμάρτητος ὑπὲρ ἀσεβῶν
ἀποθανεῖται is a Christian interpretation.

² W. Morel, *Rheinisches Museum NF* 75 (1926), pp. 106-114
traces the speech back to thoughts of Poseidonios.

³ cf. Letter of Aristeas 212, τὴν ἀδικίαν τοῦ ζῆν στέρησιν εἶναι.

(c) *The expectation of an eternal life after death* is universally accepted in Hellenistic Judaism. It is contrasted with the παρὸν ζῆν (II Macc. vii.9), the νῦν βίος (IV Macc. xii.19), as the ζωὴ αἰώνιος (IV Macc. xv.3; Ps. Sol. iii.16; Test. Asher v.2, etc., cf. Ps. Sol. xiii.9: ἡ γὰρ ζωὴ τῶν δικαίων εἰς τὸν αἰῶνα; Wisd. v.15 δίκαιοι δὲ εἰς τὸν αἰῶνα ζῶσιν) or ἀέναος ζωή (II Macc. vii.35). Nor is ζωή by itself uncommon (Test. Judah xxv.1 (xxv.4, as also xxiv.4 may be a Christian addition)); as also ζῆν alone (Ps. Sol. xv.15). So ἀθανασία is also found (Wisd. iii.4, xv.3 εἰδέναι σου τὸ κράτος ῥίζα ἀθανασίας; otherwise iv.1). The idea of the heavenly existence is the same as in Palestinian Judaism [1] where the Greek philosophical ideas have not been taken over, as in Jos. *Bell* 7.344, 346: the soul freed from its earthly burden μακαρίας ἰσχύος καὶ πανταχόθεν ἀκωλύτον μέτεχει δυνάμεως. On the other hand the Palestinian concept of resurrection is only partially taken over by Hellenistic Judaism [2] and the doctrine of the immortality of the soul is frequently substituted which is the result of the influence of the dualistic Hellenistic anthropology.[3] Connected with this the idea of Sheol

[1] cf. p. 46 and Bousset-Gressmann, pp. 277 f. where Hellenistic and Palestinian material is brought together. Also the characteristic combination of φῶς and ζωή is found in Sib.II.316, angels will lead the souls of the righteous εἰς φῶς . . . καὶ εἰς ζωὴν ἀμέριμνον. Also the idea of the winning of eternal life as a victory, IV Macc. vii.3, xvii.15; Wisd. iv.2.

[2] II Macc. vii.14 ἀνάστασις εἰς ζωήν; ἀναστῆναι εἰς ζωήν Ps. Sol. iii.16; Test. Jud. xxv.1 (xxv.4 ἐξυπνισθῆναι εἰς ζωήν a Christian interpolation?); cf. II Macc. vii.9, God εἰς αἰώνιον ἀναβιώσιν ζωῆς ἡμᾶς ἀναστήσει; vii.23 τὸ πνεῦμα καὶ τὴν ζωὴν ὑμῖν πάλιν ἀποδίδωσιν.

[3] Dualistic anthropology in Wisd. viii.19 f., ix.15, cf. Bousset-Gressmann, pp. 400-402. The soul is seen as immortal in Jos. *Bell.* 7.347 f. (cf. A. Schlatter, *Wie sprach Jos. von Gott?* (1910), pp. 47-49). For Philo see below pp. 52 ff. Also the ψυχή (of the godly) is to be seen as ἀθάνατος, IV Macc. xiv.6, xviii.23.

is abandoned in favour of the idea of a reward which follows immediately after death and belongs to the next world.[1]

4. Philo

(a) Life. In Philo's ζωή-concept the influence of the different traditions at work in Hellenism asserts itself strongly.[2] On one occasion he uses ζωή in the Greek and especially in the Stoic sense of the physical force of life, which is at work in the ψυχή and is common to man and the other ζῷα,[3] and, on the model of Aristotle, distinguishes the λογική δύναμις from the ζωτική. The former is the possession of man alone since (according to Gen. ii.7) God breathed πνεῦμα into him.[4] If physical life is a θνητή ζωή,[5] God's πνεῦμα gave the δύναμις ἀληθινῆς ζωῆς to the νοῦς so that (according to Gen. ii.7) man became εἰς ψυχὴν ... νοεράν καὶ ζῶσαν ὄντως.[6]

The concept of the ἀληθινὴ ζωή[7] is seen first and foremost in terms of the Greek and especially Stoic tradition as a matter of the 'how' of life, a mode of the

---

[1] For retribution immediately on death, cf. Wisd. iii.1 ff., Bousset-Gressmann, pp. 284 f., 269 f.

[2] Besides the literature on Philo of J. Grill, *Untersuchungen über die Entstehung des vierten Ev.* I (1902), pp. 206-211. E. von Schrenck pp. 17-31.

[3] *Spec. Leg.* IV.123. cf. Leisegang Index (cf. p. 106, n. 2).

[4] *Det. Pot. Ins.* 80-84; *Op. Mund.* 73 where Philo has besides ζῷα ἄλογα and human existence also ζῷα νοερά, which is of the planets. Cf. *Plant.* 12; *Gig.* 7 f. where the ἀήρ is filled with invisible ζῷα (the ψυχαί).

[5] *Fug.* 39, 59; *Virt.* 53, 76.

[6] *Leg. All.* I.32, 35; *Rer. Div. Her.* 56; *Spec. Leg.* IV.123.

[7] Other expressions: ἀληθὴς ζωή (of σπουδαῖος) *Poster. C.* 45; *Migr. Abr.* 21; *Mut. Nom.* 213. ἀληθὴς βίος *Leg. All.* II.93. ἡ πρὸς ἀλήθειαν ζωή *Congr.* 87. ἡ ἀψευδεστάτη ζωή *Mut. Nom.* 213; *Rer. Div. Her.* 201. ζῆν ἀψευδῶς. Θεῷ ζῆν: *Mut. Nom.* 213, *Rer. Div. Her.* 111. ἡ θεοῦ or κατὰ θεὸν ζωή, *Poster. C.* 69.

βίος.¹ It is the way in which life is led in ἀρετή,² in σωφροσύνη,³ in the knowledge of God.⁴ So the ὄντως ζῆν is contrasted with κατ' αἴσθησιν ζωή;⁵ just as the μετὰ σώματος ζωή is set over against the τέλειος βίος.⁶ Thus Philo can quite simply give the definition: *goodness and virtue is life (ζωή), evil and wickedness is death (Fug.* 58), and can in this sense provide a variation of a saying of Heraclitus (fr 62): *some people are dead while living, and some alive while dead (Fug.* 55; *Leg. All* I.108). If in pursuing the thought logically there are *two kinds of men (Rer. Div. Her.* 57), Philo nevertheless distinguishes three kinds of ζωή in *Rer. Div. Her.* 45 f.: *Now there are three kinds of life, one looking Godwards, another looking to created things, another on the border-line, a mixture of the other two.*⁷

For Philo, however, the life in the σῶμα is not only considered as of less value when it is dominated by pleasures, but it is already bad in itself and is a fetter

---

¹ Philo can use ζωή and βίος, or ζῆν and βιοῦν, indifferently, (βίος in the Greek sense, e.g. *Vit. Mos.* I. 29) and he talks also of the ἀθάνατος (or θνητὸς) and ἄφθαρτος βίος of the wise, *Det. Pot. Ins.* 49; *Ebr.* 152; *Fug.* 58 f.; *Spec. Leg.* I. 345, etc. The θνητὸς βίος is to be seen as οὐ βίος ἀλλά χρόνος, *Op. Mund.* 156. For ἀβίωτος βίος cf. Leisegang (cf. p. 106, n. 2).

² *Leg. All.* I. 35; III.52; *participating in virtue is the happiness of rich life (ζωή). Mut. Nom.* 213; *for the life (βίος) of virtue is life (ζωή) in its truest form.* Thus the ξύλον τῆς ζωῆς (Gen. ii.9) is the ἀρετή, *Op. Mund.* 154, etc.

³ *Leg. All.* II.93.　　　　　⁴ *Spec. Leg.* I.345.

⁵ *Rer. Div. Her.* 52-62. Here also are distinguished two kinds of ψυχή as in *Spec. Leg.* IV.123. Corresponding to this Philo distinguishes the πνεῦμα θεοῦ as the physical power of life (ὁ ῥέων ἀὴρ ἀπὸ γῆς) from the divine πνεῦμα as the ἀκήρατος (pure) ἐπιστήμη *Gig.* 22-27.

⁶ *Abr.* 271. That for the τέλειος βίος length of life is not important (so also *Fug.* 56 f.) is a Stoic concept. Cf. E. Benz, *Das Todesproblem in der stoischen Philosophie* (1929), pp. 103 ff.

⁷ cf. *Gig.* 60 f.; *Somn.* I. 150-152; II.234.

for the soul.[1] At these points the Orphic and the Platonic images of the body as a δεσμός and a σῆμα [2] are used and the σῶμα is called the συμφυὴς νεκρὸς ἡμῶν.[3] Thus Philo can describe even the soul of the philosophers: *who from first to last study to die to the life of the body, that a higher existence immortal and incorporeal, in the presence of him who is himself immortal and uncreated, may be their portion* (*Gig.* 14). The wise man: *desires to live to the soul alone and not to the body* (*Vit. Mos.* I.29). The essential ζωή pursuant to this dualistic conception is not the virtuous way of life but a life outside the body and can, indeed, either be thought of as the life of blessedness following bodily death or as the ecstatic experiences of the vision of God. But these ideas are not clearly distinguished and the terminology is not sharply differentiated: (1) the good, who lead the βίος μετ' ἀρετῆς, *live for ever* (ζῆν εἰς ἀεί) *even if cut off from their partnership with the body* (*Fug.* 55) [4] and in this sense Philo calls the ζωή (or the βίος) of the wise man ἀθάνατος [5] or ἀίδιος,[6] αἰώνιος,[7] ἀφθάρτος,[8] without its

---

[1] *Leg. All.* II.57; III.151; *Det. Pot. Ins.* 158; *Ebr.* 152; *Rer. Div. Her.* 68. Cf. δεσμωτήριον *Leg. All.* III.21; *Ebr.* 101; *Migr. Abr.* 9; *Rer. Div. Her.* 85; *Somn.* I.139.

[2] *Leg. All.* I.108; *Spec. Leg.* IV.188. Cf. τύμβος *Deus Imm.* 150; *Somn.* I.139.

[3] *Gig.* 15. Cf. *Leg. All.* III.69, II.72. Cf. *Migr. Abr.* 21; *Somn.* II.237; I.148. The σῶμα and its ἐπιθυμίαι prevent the ἀνάληψις and χρῆσις of the ἀρετή, this one must ἀλλοτριοῦσθαι *Leg. All.* I.103 f.; *Ebr.* 71. For the σῶμα not only suffers physical death but threatens the ψυχή with the death of the κακία *Leg. All.* I.105-108. Cf. also *Spec. Leg.* IV. 114 f. The same thought in Jos. *Bell.* 7.344.

[4] *Plant.* 37, *Conf. Ling.* 161; *Vit. Mos.* II. 288. Cf. E. Bréhier, *Les Idées philosophiques et religieuses de Philon d'Alexandrie* (1907), pp. 240-242. H. Windisch, *Die Frömmigkeit Philos* (1909), p. 6.

[5] *Op. Mund.* 155 f.; *Poster. C.* 39, 68 f. (λογικὴ καὶ ἀθάνατος ζωή); *Plant.* 44; *Fug.* 55; *Spec. Leg.* 1.31, 345.   [6] *Fug.* 97.

[7] *Fug.* 78.   [8] *Det. Pot. Ins.* 49; *Gig.* 14; *Fug.* 59.

being possible to tell whether it is a real or ideal eternity in the Greek sense that is meant,¹ just as also ἀποθνήσκειν τὸν μετὰ σωμάτων βίον does not necessarily mean bodily death but can mean the philosophical life;² (2) on the other hand the ἀθάνατος καὶ μακαρία ζωή which has left θνήτος βίος is, in *Vit. Cont.* 12 f., the ecstatic vision, as also the *divine life of reasonable and happy souls* in *Ebr.* 99 f.³

Ζωή is not used of God himself, although in *Decal.* 67 it is true he is described as ἀεὶ ζῶν. He is ζωῆς αἴτιος (*Op. Mund.* 30; cf. *Aet. Mund.* 106) and that both in the sense of the physical and the spiritual ζωή (*Fug.* 198), but *Matter is a dead thing, but God is something more than life, an ever-flowing spring of living, as he himself says* (Jer. ii.13) (*ibid.*). Philo can speak of his βίυς by describing it as *eternity which is the archetype and pattern of time* (*Deus Imm.* 32).

(b) *Death.* In Philo the Stoic-Neoplatonic usage is frequently met, which corresponds to his use of ζωή (cf. pp. 52-5). Πρὸς ἀλήθειαν τεθνάναι stands in contrast to the ἀψευδῶς ζῆν.⁴ It is the state of corruption due to the αἰσθητά σώματα and πράγματα which are

---

¹ Both are expressed in *Spec. Leg.* II.262, the ἀρετή is promised *Salvation from death given by prolonged vitality and agelong life which you will keep thriving even while in the body, if you live with a soul purged clean of all impurity.* Philo can even speak, as a Greek, of living on for ever through immortal deeds, *Spec. Leg.* IV.169.

² *Gig.* 14. See pp. 55 f.

³ cf. *Mut. Nom.* 209 f.; *Somn.* II. 250. This ἀνάκλησις τοῦ προφήτου is characterised as a 'second birth' in *Quaest. in Ex.* II.46. The text and its associated references in *Quaest. in Ex.* in R. Reitzenstein, *Die Vorgeschichte der christlichen Taufe* (1929), pp. 107-119. On the influence of the ideas of the mystery cults, Bréhier, *op. cit.* pp. 242-246. The ideas of entrance into life after death and the ecstasy are uniquely combined in *Vit. Mos.* II.291.

⁴ *Rer. Div. Her.* 201.

'not living'.¹ Thus Cain is continually dying ² during his bodily life because he has become corrupt as a result of λύπη and φόβος. Likewise out of ἡδονή grows θάνατος.³ The wicked are ἔτι ζῶντες νεκροί.⁴

In contrast with this, bodily death, which is χωρισμὸς ψυχῆς ἀπὸ σώματος⁵ is an ἀγαθόν or an ἀδιάφορον.⁶ In this sense Philo distinguishes a διττὸς θάνατος.⁷ In practice, however, he uses the words ζωή and θάνατος in a threefold sense,⁸ since he also speaks of the ascetic ἀποθνήσκειν θνητῆς ζωῆς; it is just this that corresponds to the attainment of the ἄφθαρτος βίος.⁹ *For the birth of good practices is the death of base* (*Deus Imm.* 123). In this Philo varies the Platonic μελετᾶν ἀποθνήσκειν and describes the souls of the genuine philosophers: in words already quoted (*Gig.* 14, cf. *Gig.* 56).¹⁰ Thus just as real ζωή for Philo (cf. pp. 52 f.) is not only the virtuous life in ideal eternity but also everlasting life in time, so also, of course, real θάνατος is eternal destruction.¹¹

---

¹ *Rer. Div. Her.* 242; *Gig.* 15; cf. *Leg. All.* I.108. Thus νεκροφορεῖν of the ψυχή which bears the νεκρὸν σῶμα, *Leg. All.* III.69, 74; *Agric.* 25, etc. Cf. p. 53.

² Ζῆν ἀποθνήσκοντα ἀεὶ *Praem. Poen.* 70 f., and there too the paradox θάνατος ἀθάνατος, cf. *Poster. C.* 44 f., ἀεὶ τὸν πρὸς ἀρετὴν βίον θνήσκοντα. In this sense the variation of the saying of Heraclitus (fr. 62. cf. p. 53).   ³ *Agric.* 98.

⁴ *Somn.* II.66; *Rer. Div. Her.* 290; *Spec. Leg.* I.345.

⁵ *Leg. All.* I.105, etc. Cf. Leisegang s. v. θάνατος 1.

⁶ *Praem. Poen.* 70.

⁷ *Leg. All.* I.105; *Praem. Poen.* 70; cf. Benz 95 ff.

⁸ He can even occasionally play in a yet different way with the word θάνατος, *Conf. Ling.* 36 f. on *Ex.* xiv.30

⁹ *Fug.* 59, *Det. Pot. Ins.* 49.

¹⁰ Occasionally (as with ζωή) there is a dualistic idea which goes further than the Stoics (e.g. *Leg. All.* I.108) where a saying of Heraclitus is explained.

¹¹ Ἀίδιος θάνατος, *Poster. C.* 39, cf. *Plant.*37, 45; *Migr. Abr.*189, etc.

IV. LIFE IN THE NEW TESTAMENT

1. *Natural life*

In the New Testament ζωή and ζῆν are used first and foremost of the natural life of man.[1] It has its antithesis and its end in natural death;[2] it is transient [3] and has only a limited extent in time;[4] it moves and is active.[5] It is realised in that the living person can effect something. This is evident both in that, as in the Old Testament, 'to live' can be used to mean 'to be in a good state of health' (Mark v.23; John iv.50) [6] and also, antithetically, in phrases where something ineffective is described as νεκρόν, such as ἁμαρτία in Rom. vii.8, ἔργα which do not achieve their object,[7] πίστις without works [8] and false gods.[9] It is shown also in the so-called figurative usage, according to which an attitude or action that is sure of its power and effect is called 'living'; words,[10] hope (I Peter i.3), sacrifice

---

[1] As in the OT the natural man or Adam can be described as ψυχὴ ζῶσα I Cor. xv.45; all living creatures can be described as πᾶσα ψυχὴ ζωῆς Rev. xvi.3; ψυχή can be used as synonymous with ζωή Mark viii.35, etc. Cf. Luke xii.15, 20.

[2] Phil. i.20: εἴτε διὰ ζωῆς εἴτε διὰ θανάτου, II Tim. i.10, etc.

[3] James iv.14 and parallels in M. Dibelius, *Jakobusbrief* (⁷1921) and H. Windisch, *Jakobusbrief* (²1930).

[4] Rom. vii.1-3: ... ἐφ' ὅσον χρόνον ζῇ .... I Cor. vii.39; Heb. ii.15: διὰ παντὸς τοῦ ζῆν; ix.17; Luke i.75, ii.36; I Clem. xxv.2; Barn. iv.9, x.6, etc. Also βιοῦν and βίος I Peter iv.2, 3. As in the OT ζωή and ἡμέραι are synonymous Heb. vii.3, 'days of life', Herm. v. IV. 2.5; 5.2, etc.

[5] Acts xvii.28: ζῶμεν καὶ κινούμεθα.

[6] The aorist of ζῆν is used for recovering health, Mark v.23, etc.

[7] Heb. ix.14; Herm. s. IX.21.2.

[8] James ii.17, 20 (variant reading), 26, cf. Rev. iii.1 f.

[9] Did. vi.3; II Clem. iii.1.

[10] Acts vii.38; Heb. iv.12; John vi.63, 68; Herm. s. IX.21.2.

(Rom. xii.1). This usage is not really figurative [1] since the power to act is an essential part of life itself. This life is a treasure, the highest good in fact (Mark viii.36 f.), and for that reason the miraculous power of Jesus is called on to save life in danger (Mark v.23; John iv.47 ff., etc.) or to call back what has passed away (Matt. ix.18, etc.). The criminal may no longer live (Acts xxii.22, xxv.24, xxviii.4) and the greatest affliction is ἐξαπορηθῆναι καὶ τοῦ ζῆν (II Cor. i.8) (cf. p. 92).

Human life is maintained [2] but not guaranteed [3] by food, in the same way as it is not dependent on food but on the πνεῦμα (ζωῆς), which does not mean the cosmic vital force in the Stoic sense, but the power bestowed by God in the Old Testament sense.[4] For ζωή is peculiar to God as the living one (ζῶν),[5] i.e. not only as the one who has ζωή within him originally (John v.26), who lives eternally [6] and who alone possesses

---

[1] One can talk of a figurative use where the noun characterised as living is used metaphorically: ὁδὸς ζῶσα Heb. x.20. λίθος ζῶν I Pet. ii.4 f. On the other hand, of course, as in the OT. flowing water is called 'living'. Did vii.1 f.

[2] Matt. iv.4 and parallels; Luke xii.15; I Cor. ix.14 (ἐκ τοῦ εὐαγγελίου ζῆν); Barn. vi.17. That is why βίος is also used for 'livelihood', Mark xii.44; Luke viii.43, xv.12, 30. So also ζωή Herm. s. IX.26. 2. βιωτικός describes the things or thoughts which concern the livelihood, I Cor. vi.3 f.; Luke xxi.34: μερίμναις βιωτικαῖς cf. Philo Vit. Mos. II.158: βιωτικαί χρεῖαι. Death and hunger belong together, Rev. vi.8, xviii.8.

[3] Matt. iv.4 and parallels; Luke xii.15.

[4] Rev. xi.11, which expresses the matter in Greek style but refers to Isa. xlii.5; Acts xvii.25: διδοὺς πᾶσιν ζωὴν καὶ πνοήν. Cf. Spirit of God (1960) in this series.

[5] God as ζῶν, as in the OT: Rom. ix.26; Matt. xvi.16; xxvi.63; Acts xiv.15; Ign.Phld. i.2; II Clem. xx.2; Herm. v. II.3.2, etc. Cf. the enlarged oath formula in I Clem. lviii.2 following Isa. xlix.18; Rom. xiv.11.

[6] Rev. iv.9 f.: τῷ ζῶντι εἰς τοὺς αἰῶνας τῶν αἰώνων; x.6, xv.7; cf. Ecclus. xviii.1.

ἀθανασία (I Tim. vi.16) but, above all, the one who can quicken and put to death.[1] Since he quickens by his spirit, the πνεῦμα can be described as ζωοποιοῦν.[2] Thus God is Lord over life and death,[3] just as he is the judge of the living and the dead.[4]

Attributing ζωή to God in this way is, nevertheless, not the same as primitive mythology in which ζωή, seen as a natural phenomenon, would be traced back to a metaphysical αἰτία (characteristic). It is rather man's absolute dependence upon God and the transcendence of God's existence that find expression here. For that reason ζωή is never looked at or examined as an observable phenomenon, but, as among the Greeks, it is seen here that life consists in the manner in which life is led. Thus ζωή can be qualified by adverbs and adverbial phrases as 'living a particular kind of life'.[5] In this sense βίος (cf. p. 23) can be used instead of

---

[1] Rom. iv.17: τοῦ ζωοποιοῦντος τοὺς νεκρούς (cf. II Cor. i.9); I Tim. vi.13: τοῦ ζωογονοῦντος (variant ζωοποιοῦντος) τὰ πάντα; John v.21, vi.57. God as ἀποκτείνων καὶ ζῆν ποιῶν: I Clem. lix.3 (also R. Knopf, ad loc.) cf. Matt. x.28 and parallels.

[2] I Cor. xv.45; John vi.63; cf. Herm. s. IX.14. 3.

[3] Luke xii.20; II Cor. i.9; James iv.15 (on this M. Dibelius, Jakobusbrief (⁷1921), and H. Windisch, Jakobusbrief (²1930).

[4] I Peter iv.5. Transferred to Christ (Rom. xiv.9); Acts x.42; II Tim. iv.1; Barn. vii.2; II Clem. i.1; Pol. ii.1.

[5] ζῆν ἀσώτως: Luke xv.13. ἐθνικῶς contrasted with Ἰουδαϊκῶς Gal. ii.14. εὐσεβῶς II Tim. iii.12; Titus ii.12. πανούργως Herm. m. III.3. Acts xxvi.5: κατὰ τὴν ἀκριβεστάτην αἵρεσιν τῆς ἡμετέρας θρησκείας ἔζησα Φαρισαῖος. Also in Ignatius ζῆν κατὰ Ἰουδαϊσμόν Mg. viii.1; κατὰ χριστιανισμόν Mg. x.1; κατὰ κυριακήν (opposite σαββατίζειν) Mg. ix.1; κατὰ χριστὸν Ἰησοῦν Mg. viii.2; Phld. iii.2; κατὰ ἄνθρωπον or ἀνθρώπους Tr. ii.1; Rom. viii.1; κατὰ θεόν Eph. viii.1; Ditt. Syll.³ 910 AB. κατὰ σάρκα Rom. viii.12 (also Dg. v.8). κατὰ ἀλήθειαν Ign. Eph. vi.2. In NT: ζῆν ἐν αὐτῇ (τῇ ἁμαρτίᾳ) Rom. vi.2; ἐν αὐτοῖς (vices) Col. iii.7; ἐν κόσμου Col. ii.20; ἐν πίστει Gal. ii.20.

ζωή.¹ But the peculiarly Greek βίος-concept has not been developed. The reason for this is that ζωή is said not to attain its intrinsic value in a βίος, but is responsible before God the judge (cf. p. 59). Man, and especially the believer, is to live his life not for himself, but for God or for the κύριος.² If he were to want to live to himself, he would live for sin and death;³ his life is subject to the question of its origin and destiny.

2. Real life as generally understood in the New Testament

Death (cf. ch. V) is no more understood as a natural phenomenon than ζωή. It is not a matter of course or inevitable, but the punishment for sin. That means, however, that part of the concept of life in the New Testament is its indestructibility. In this sense ζωή is peculiar to God (cf. p. 58), and this ζωή is real ζωή, over against which the ζωή subject to death cannot really be considered as ζωή, but is distinguished from the real life by being temporary ⁴ or ζῆν ἐν σαρκί.⁵ So men who are involved in natural life can, although they are physically alive, be described as dead.⁶ Real,

---

¹ I Tim. ii.2: ἵνα ἤρεμον καὶ ἡσύχιον βίον διάγωμεν. In Luke viii.14; II Tim. ii.4(?); I John ii.16: βίος without adverbial or adjectival qualification, seems to mean the 'manner of life'; βίωσις is used in that sense in Acts xxvi.4. Ζωή is used for 'manner of life' without further definition in Herm. m. XI.7. 16.

² Rom. xiv.7 f.; II Cor. v.15; Gal. ii.19; cf. I Pet. ii.24 (τῇ δικαιοσύνῃ). ζῆν τῷ θεῷ which is frequent in Hermas (e.g. s. VIII.11.1 f.) refers not to the 'manner of life' but to 'having life in God' (cf. p. 62, n. 6). ³ II Cor. v.15; Rom. vi.2.

⁴ I Cor. xv.19: εἰ ἐν τῇ ζωῇ ταύτῃ ἐν χριστῷ ἠλπικότες ἐσμέν μόνον. I Tim. iv.8: ἐπαγγελίαν ἔχουσα ζωῆς τῆς νῦν καὶ τῆς μελλούσης. ⁵ Gal. ii.20; Phil. i.22.

⁶ Matt. viii.22 and parallels; Luke xv. 24, 32; Col. ii.13 and Eph. ii.1, 5: ὑμᾶς νεκροὺς ὄντας τοῖς παραπτώμασιν..., Eph. v.14: ἀνάστα ἐκ τῶν νεκρῶν. Rev. iii.1: ὅτι ζῇς καὶ νεκρὸς εἶ. I Tim. v.6: ζῶσα τέθνηκε. See John v.21, 25, cf. II Clem. i.6: ὁ βίος ἡμῶν ὅλος ἄλλο οὐδὲν ἦν εἰ μὴ θάνατος. According to Herm.

true [1] ζωή is seen primarily as the future life after death, as the μέλλουσα.[2] Because the future ζωή is the true one, it can, as already in Judaism (cf. pp. 45, n. 1; 51), be called simply ζωή, without an attributive,[3] just as ζῆν can also be used in this sense without being qualified more specifically.[4] As something indestructible it is often described as αἰώνιος;[5] as deliverance from death it is

s. IX.16. 1 ff. man is dead before baptism. This is a formal parallel to the late Greek Stoic usage. But there is a real difference in that real ζωή is not to be understood in an ideal sense. Cf. also Eph. iv.18 (ἀπηλλοτριωμένοι τῆς ζωῆς τοῦ θεοῦ) with Philo Poster. C. 29 (ἀνάγκη τὸν ἀλόγως βιοῦντα τῆς τοῦ θεοῦ ζωῆς ἀπεσχοινίσθαι (to separate oneself)). The influence of the Greek usage shows itself in contrast in Did. iv.8: εἰ γὰρ ἐν τῷ ἀθανάτῳ κοινωνοί ἐστε, πόσῳ μᾶλλον ἐν τοῖς θνητοῖς (i.e. in earthly goods, cf. on the other hand Rom. xv.27; I Cor. ix.11; Barn. xix.8), at any rate in Dg. vii.1: θνητὴ ἐπίνοια; I Clem. xxxvi.2: ἀθάνατος γνῶσις.

[1] ζωή ἀληθινή: Ign. Eph. vii.2. τὸ ἀληθινὸν ζῆν: xi.1; Tr. ix.2; Sm. iv.1. τὸ ἀληθῶς ζῆν: Dg. x.7. In John ἀληθινός is never an attribute of ζωή, but the combination of ἀλήθεια and ζωή (John xiv.6) shows the same ideas as the combination of ζῶν and ἀληθινός as predicates of God in I Thess. i.9. Once in I Tim. vi.19 the Greek concept of ὄντως ζωή approaches that found in Dg. x.7 as ὄντως θάνατος.

[2] I Tim. iv. 8. τὸ προκείμενον ζῆν Ign. Eph. xvii.1.

[3] Mark ix.43, 45; Matt. vii.14, xviii.8 ff.; I Peter iii.7, 10; II Peter i.3; Did. ix.3; Barn. ii.10; Herm. v. I.1.9; Dg. ix.6. ἀνάστασις ζωῆς John v.29; Mart. Pol. xiv.2 (cf. p. 51, n. 2). In this sense one can also speak of στέφανος τῆς ζωῆς Rev. ii.10; James i.12 (cf. p. 47, n. 1) and of ξύλον τῆς ζωῆς Rev. ii.7; xxii.2, 14, 19 (cf. p. 46, n. 1).

[4] Rom. i.17, viii.13; I Thess. v.10; Luke x.28; Heb. xii.9; Barn. vi.17, etc. So of the Christians: ἡμεῖς οἱ ζῶντες II Clem. iii.1. Perhaps οἱ ζῶντες was an old description the Christians used of themselves. F. J. Dölger, 'Ιχθύς I (1910), pp. 167 f. E. Peterson, 'Εἷς θεός (1926), pp. 18 f.

[5] Mark x.17; Matt. xix.16, 29, xxv.46; Rom. ii.7, v.21, vi.22 f.; Gal. vi.8; I Tim. i.16; vi.12; Titus i.2, iii.7; Jude 21; Acts xiii.46, 48; John iii.15 f., iv.14, vi.27; Herm. v. II.3. 2; Mart. Pol. xiv.2, etc. (cf. p. 45, n. 1; 51). Ζῆν εἰς τὸν αἰῶνα Barn. viii.5, ix.2, xi.10 f. καινότης ἀιδίου ζωῆς Ign. Eph. xix.3. ἐπουράνιος ζωή II Clem. xx.5.

occasionally with σωτηρία.[1] It is something which one will inherit,[2] receive,[3] earn,[4] something into which one will enter.[5] By his behaviour now man can become worthy of ζωή,[6] so that the New Testament, like Judaism, can speak of the 'way of life'[7] and of repentance that leads to life.[8] But man is in control of this ζωή as little as he is of natural life. Just as the latter was given him by God's creative act, so the former is given him in the resurrection, if God awakens him; the idea of the immortality of the soul is completely absent.[9] The

---

[1] Ign. Eph. xviii.1; II Clem. xix.1. (ζῆν and σωθῆναι of recovering Mark v.23), cf. Rom. v.10. Combination of ζωή and ἀφθαρσία II Tim. i.10; Ign. Pol. ii.3; cf. Rom. ii.7; Mart. Pol. xiv.2; II Clem. xiv.5. According to I Clem. xxxv.2, ζωὴ ἐν ἀθανασίᾳ is first among the δῶρα of God.

[2] κληρονομεῖν Mark x.17; Matt. xix.29; Luke x.25; Titus iii.7; I Peter iii.7; Herm.v. III.8. 4, etc.

[3] (ἀπο) λαμβάνειν Mark x.30; Luke xviii.30; II Clem. viii.6, cf. Matt. xix.16.

[4] περιποιεῖσθαι Herm. m. III. 5, s. VI. 5. 7.

[5] εἰσελθεῖν εἰς τὴν ζωὴν Mark ix.43 ff.; Matt. xviii.8 f., xix.17.

[6] Mark x.17, 30 and parallels; Matt. xxv.46; Rom. ii.7, vi.22 f.; Gal. vi.8; John v.29, xii.25; II Clem. viii.4, x.1, etc. Luke x.28: τοῦτο ποίει καὶ ζήσῃ, often similarly in Hermas, mostly with the addition τῷ θεῷ Herm. v. III. 8. 5; m. IV. 2. 3 f. (cf. p. 60, n. 2); cf. Mart. Pol. xiv.1: τῶν δικαίων, οἳ ζῶσιν ἐνώπιόν σου (God).

[7] Matt. vii.13 f. (also E. Klostermann, *Kommentar zum Matthäusevangelium* (²1927), A. Schlatter, *Kommentar zum Matthäusevangelium* (1929)—cf. p. 19 and p. 43, n. 4); Did. i.1 f., iv.14; Barn. xix.1 f., xx.1; Herm. s. V. 6. 3 (αἱ τρίβοι τῆς ζωῆς). Differently in Acts xi.18 following Ps. xvi (LXX xv).11.

[8] Acts xi.18; Herm. s. VI. 2. 3; VIII. 6. 6.

[9] The idea of the immortality of the soul is found first in connection with the dualistic Hellenistic psychology, Dg. vi. Just as I Cor. xv and Acts xvii.18, 32 show the strangeness of the Christian belief in resurrection to the Greek hearers, so the proof of this belief is the main difficulty of the Apologists, which is even seen in I Clem. xxiv-xxvii. J. Geffcken, *Zwei griech Apologeten* (1907), pp. 235 ff., 244 f. For the Apologists ψυχή is actually ἀθάνατος but through sin it has fallen under death (Just. *Dial.*

sovereignty of God is expressed by such Old Testament phrases as ὅσοι ἦσαν τεταγμένοι εἰς ζωὴν αἰώνιον (Acts xiii.48) [1] and by the concept, originally deterministic, of the book or books of life, in which those who are destined for life are listed,[2] even if the original determinism of the idea is set aside.[3]

3. The assurance of life in Jesus Christ

Up to this point the primitive Christian view corresponds to the Jewish one in substance and expression. The decisive difference, however, is that God's future act of resurrection is founded, according to the New Testament, on the raising of Jesus Christ from the dead. That he who was dead is alive is the message of Easter [4] and the core of the Christian kerugma,[5] and this life is indeed an eternal, indestructible one.[6] Death is thereby robbed of its power (cf. pp. 93 ff.).

Thus, belief in the possibility of a future ζωή is not based simply on the idea of God, although even this can motivate the idea of resurrection (Mark xii.27 and parallels). It means in fact that the idea of God is

cxxiv.4; Tatian xiii.1, xv.4), and will only be really ἀθάνατος through the resurrection (Just. Dial. xlvi.7, lxix.7, cxvii.3; Tatian xiii.1, xv.4). But Justin can make the difference from the immortality of the soul plain (Dial. iv 5; Apol. xliv.9). Cf. L. Atzberger, Geschichte der christl. Eschatologie innerhalb der vornicänischen Zeit (1896), pp. 116-121.

[1] cf. Herm. v. IV. 3. 5: οἱ ἐκλελεγμένοι εἰς ζωὴν αἰώνιον.

[2] Rev. xiii.8, xvii.8; I Clem. liii.4, following Ex. xxxii.31 f.; Herm. v. I. 3.2.; s. II. 9. Cf. TWNT I, pp. 613 ff.

[3] cf. Rev. iii.5, xx.12, 15, xxi.27.

[4] Luke xxiv. 9, 23; Acts i.3.

[5] Rom. vi.10, xiv.9 II Cor. xiii.4; Acts xxv. 19; Heb. vii.8, 25; Rev. i.18, ii.8. Differently formulated in Rom. x.9; I Cor. xv.3 ff. Cf. Ign. Mg. ix.1; Tr. ix.2.

[6] εἰς τοὺς αἰῶνας τῶν αἰώνων Rev. i.18. ἀκατάλυτος Heb. vii.16. Cf. Rom. vi.10: ὃ γὰρ ἀπέθανεν, τῇ ἁμαρτίᾳ ἀπέθανεν ἐφάπαξ, ὃ δὲ ζῇ, ζῇ τῷ θεῷ; cf. the commentaries.

understood more radically; the distance between man and God, caused by sin, is seen more profoundly; man's claim is denied more radically. If God gives new and true life, he does so on the strength of his unpredictable, unexpected, gracious act of salvation, without which we would be lost.[1] Therefore, hope [2] is based on the belief in this act of salvation: ὁ δίκαιος ἐκ πίστεως ζήσεται.[3] Whoever believes in Jesus will have life.[4] It is Jesus then who has brought ζωή and ἀφθαρσία to light (II Tim. i.10); he is the ἀρχηγὸς τῆς ζωῆς (Acts iii.15); it is through his life, which overcame death, that we shall be saved (Rom. v.10).[5] He is our ζωή, and, if it is one day granted to us, it is now hidden with him in God (Col. iii.3 f.). Life is 'in him'.[6] He is the ἀνάστασις and the ζωή (John xi.25), the ὁδός, ἀλήθεια and ζωή (John xiv.6), so that in I John v.20 it can be said of him: οὗτός ἐστιν ὁ ἀληθινὸς θεὸς καὶ ζωὴ αἰώνιος.[7]

---

[1] God's χάρις (Rom. v.15, 17; I Peter iii.7) or Christ's ἔλεος (Jude 21) give life.

[2] cf. Hope (1963) in this series.

[3] Following Hab. ii.4; Rom. i.17; Gal. iii.11; Heb. x.38. Cf. Titus i.1 f.; Barn, i.6: ζωῆς ἐλπίς as ἀρχὴ καὶ τέλος πίστεως ἡμῶν (cf. H. Windisch, ad loc.), viii.5: οἱ ἐλπίζοντες ἐπ' αὐτὸν ζήσονται εἰς τὸν αἰῶνα. Ign. Eph. xiv.1: πίστις and ἀγάπη as ἀρχὴ ζωῆς καὶ τέλος.

[4] Rom. vi.8 ff.; I Tim. i. 16; John iii.15 f.; cf. Acts xi.18 with xv.7-9, xiii.48 also Rom. x.9. Only the believer is ἄξιος τῆς αἰωνίου ζωῆς: Acts xiii.46.

[5] cf. also Did. ix.3: εὐχαριστοῦμεν ... ὑπὲρ τῆς ζωῆς καὶ γνώσεως, ἧς ἐγνώρισας ἡμῖν διὰ Ἰησοῦ τοῦ παιδός σου. Barn. i.4: ἐν ἐλπίδι ζωῆς αὐτοῦ, xii.5: καὶ αὐτὸς (Jesus) ζωοποιήσει. Ign. Mg. ix.2: πῶς ἡμεῖς δυνησόμεθα ζῆσαι χωρὶς αὐτοῦ, Tr. ix.2: οὗ χωρὶς τὸ ἀληθινὸν ζῆν οὐκ ἔχομεν.

[6] Rom. viii.2; II Tim. i.1; I John v.11.

[7] In Ignatius Christ is described as τὸ ἀδιάκριτον ἡμῶν ζῆν Eph. iii.2; as ἐν θανάτῳ ζωὴ ἀληθινή Eph. vii.2; as τὸ διὰ παντὸς ἡμῶν ζῆν Mg. i.2; as τὸ ἀληθινὸν ἡμῶν ζῆν Sm. iv.1.

4. *Life, future and present*

With this, however, a considerable change has taken place. For as the future ζωή is based on the redemptive event of Christ's (death and) resurrection, which is past, the decisive event has already happened, and the resurrection of the dead which is hoped for in the future is only the completion of the event, which begins in Christ, of the dawn of the new age. This change is expressed with differing clarity and consistency and by means of various concepts in the different New Testament writings, and it depends on this how far ζωή is seen as a gift of the future or a fact of the present.

In the synoptic account of the preaching of Jesus, of course, only the future ζωή is mentioned,[1] since this preaching does not yet look back on his death and resurrection as events that determine the present, and, of course, in all New Testament writings there can also be talk of the future ζωή. The question is how far the present is already seen in the light of this future ζωή. This is the case where the present is seen in a future hope, a hope that is certain because it is based on the saving event.[2] Thus, ἐλπίς itself can be described as ζῶσα (cf. p. 57), because God has borne us to it again through the resurrection of Christ (I Pet. i.3). So in the Book of Revelation only future life is mentioned (e.g. ii.7, 10, xx.4 f.) but the present is maintained by the certainty of this future.[3] In Col. iii.3 f. the way this certainty is expressed is that ζωή is already seen as present, but as still hidden in order to become revealed one day.[4] The same is to be found in the expression

---

[1] Dalman, WJ I, p. 132.
[2] cf. *Hope* (1963) in this series.
[3] Similarly Acts xi.18, xiii.46-48; I Peter iii.7, 10; Jude 21.
[4] See p. 64, n. 3 on the connection of ζωή and ἐλπίς.

that ζωή is given in Jesus Christ (II Tim. i.1, cf. p. 64, n. 6). So in I Tim. vi.12 the exhortation is given to lay hold of this ζωή, which, of course, can extend into the future (I Tim. vi.19). Indeed the pastoral writers can say that ζωή is already manifest and is a fact of present reality in the proclamation of the gospel.[1]

In these instances it is often difficult to say how far, through the more or less radical reference to the present, the concept of ζωή has itself been deepened; i.e. it is difficult to say whether and how far ζωή is conceived as something to be fulfilled in the future and not merely thought of, to a greater or lesser extent, as a resumption of the ζωή possessed hitherto and interrupted by death. It is seen, of course, as being free from suffering and transience;[2] it will be in χαρά;[3] it will consist in δόξα[4] so that ζωή and δόξα can become simply synonymous.[5] However, the Jewish concept of life is not yet modified thereby, nor even in that Mark xii.25 (and parallels) expressly maintains the cessation of the limitations of earthly life (cf. p. 46).

---

[1] II Tim. i.10, imitated in II Clem. xx.5; Titus i.2 f. Without this reference Ign. Mg. ix.1: ἐν ᾗ (the κυριακὴ ἡμέρα) καὶ ἡ ζωὴ ἡμῶν ἀνέτειλεν δι' αὐτοῦ καὶ τοῦ θανάτου αὐτοῦ. In Ignatius, for whom the Eucharist is φάρμακον ἀθανασίας (Eph. xx.2) the thought of the presence of ζωή is determined by the concepts of the sacraments in the mysteries. (H. Schlier, *Religionsgeschichte. Untersuchungen zu den Ignatiusbriefen* (1929), pp. 165 ff.). With reference to the Eucharist Did. x.3 says: ἡμῖν δὲ ἐχαρίσω πνευματικὴν τροφὴν καὶ ποτὸν καὶ ζωὴν αἰώνιον διὰ τοῦ παιδός σου. In Hermas ζωή has become a present possession through baptism, v. III.3.5, s. VI.16. 2-7, as far as the author can be said to talk of the presence of life.

[2] Rev. xxi.4, etc.

[3] Matt. xxv.21, 23; I Thess. ii.19 f.; I Peter i.8.

[4] II Tim. ii.10; I Peter v.1, 4, 10, etc.

[5] cf. I Peter v.4, with James i.12; Rev. ii.10 and the connection of δόξα and ζωή II Cor. iii.6-11.

5. *Life as present reality in Paul*

(a) *The concepts used in the presentation of life as present reality*

The idea of the present reality of ζωή is expressed in a far more radical way first in Paul. For this he is able to make use not only of the Jewish eschatological concept of the dawn of the age (which, in his opinion, has already come) but also of the concepts of the Gnostic anthropos myth.[1] Through his resurrection Christ has become the second Adam, the inauguration of a new humanity, to which believers belong; he is the ἀπαρχὴ τῶν κεκοιμημένων (I Cor. xv.20, 23), the πρωτότοκος (ἐκ τῶν νεκρῶν) (Rom. viii.29, cf. Col. i.18). In this Paul can at one point have the future realisation in mind (I Cor. xv.20-22, 44-49) and at another the present, which has already become decisively new (Rom. v.12-21). Likewise he can use the πνεῦμα-concept of the mysteries and of Gnosticism to serve this idea.[2] The πνεῦμα which is given to the believer in baptism, is the earnest of the future.[3] Indeed, Paul can even express himself in Hellenistic ways as if the πνεῦμα were a miraculous substance, a possession which guarantees future resurrection (Rom. viii.11).[4] But, in fact, the πνεῦμα for him means the way the life of faith is lived in its relationship to God's act of salvation in Christ.[5] It is precisely because the relationship is formed in the way the present life is lived that he can appropriate to himself the Hellenistic πνεῦμα-concept

[1] As far as we can see, since Dan. vii, Jewish apocalyptic had taken over other motifs of the 'Anthropos Myth'.
[2] cf. *Spirit of God* (1960) in this series.
[3] ἀπαρχή: Rom. viii.23. ἀρραβών: II Cor. i.22, v.5. Cf. Gal. iv.6 f., v.5.
[4] K. Deissner, *Auferstehungshoffnung und Pneumagedanks bei Paulus* (1912). [5] cf. *Faith* (1961) in this series.

(though modified, of course, by the Old Testament idea of the spirit) and, in order to describe Christ as the one who is alive and active, can connect him so closely with the πνεῦμα that he applies to Christ what in the Old Testament is said of the spirit (II Cor. iii.17). For him ζωή is no more an idea or a hyperphysical condition than Christ is an idea or, as in Gnosticism, a cosmic power. It is rather the present historical reality of the believer. The πνεῦμα ζωοποιοῦν,[1] which he explicitly differentiates from the power of the merely natural life, the ψυχή ζῶσα (I Cor. xv.45), is in fact a present reality.[2] If, therefore, the life of resurrection also only reaches full development in the future and if ζωή is, to this extent, still an object of hope,[3] it is nevertheless in a certain sense a present reality, just as also the future δόξα is already anticipated in faith (Rom. viii.30; II Cor. iii.6-18).

(b) Life as present reality in the Word and in faith

The present reality of the ζωή is to be understood neither in the idealistic sense of Stoicism (cf. p. 25), as if it consisted in the timeless validity of a βίος κατ' ἀρετήν; nor in the Gnostic sense, as if ζωή, as a mysterious substance which guarantees ἀφθαρσία, were a possession of the believer, which comes home to him in isolated and physically static moments, moments which interrupt the flow of life; nor in the sense of Philo, who unites both these possibilities (cf. p. 52). Paul differs from the Stoic (and Philonic) conception in that the πνεῦμα is not the νοῦς in the philosophical sense, but the supernatural power of God, which is not inherent in man in his human nature,

---

[1] I Cor. xv.45; II Cor. iii.6; Rom. viii.6.

[2] J. Sickenberger, *Die Briefedeshl. Paulus an die Römer und Korinther* ([4]1932), p. 80.

[3] Rom. v.1-11, viii.12-39; I Cor. xv; II Cor. v.1-5.

which is also not, like the νοῦς, developed in the βίος. He differs from Gnosticism on the other hand in that the πνεῦμα, although represented in the forms of Gnostic concepts as a mysterious, material fluid, is in fact interpreted quite differently. The prerequisite to the receipt of πνεῦμα and ζωή is, on the one hand, the preached word, which proclaims not timeless truths dressed up as myth, but an historical event. As such, it is not the simple transmission of something that can be known and from which, as a proclamation, it could be separated, but it belongs itself to the redemptive event and gives to each individual the grace of God, which is at work in the redemptive event. Thus, in this proclaimed word, as an historical event, the presence of life can be seen. It propagates life (II Cor. ii.16, iii.6-18, v.18-20); it is the δύναμις θεοῦ εἰς σωτηρίαν (Rom. i.16); it is the λόγος ζωῆς (Phil. ii.16),[1] so that it can be said in Paul's sense that the gospel destroys death and reveals life (II Tim. i.10, cf. Titus i.2 f.). The prerequisite to the receipt of life is, on the other hand, faith, which, as obedience,[2] lays hold of the act of God and the gift of salvation that has been established in it. As death is seen as the consequence of sin, so the prerequisite to ζωή is the forgiveness of sin, the δικαιοσύνη (ἐκ) θεοῦ,[3] which confronts man in the word of the preaching.[4] Therefore, just as the ultimate meaning of the act of salvation is forgiveness, so also the ζωή that is present in the πνεῦμα is the actuality of the forgiveness of sins with all the possibilities it gives to the believer. The πνεῦμα then, is neither in the Stoic nor the Gnostic sense a possession of man. On

---

[1] cf. ῥήματα ζωῆς: Acts v.20; John vi.63, 68.

[2] cf. *Faith* (1961) in this series.

[3] cf. the relationship of Rom. v-viii to iii.21-iv.25. R. Bultmann, *Imago Dei* (1932), pp. 53-62.

[4] cf. TWNT III, pp. 682 ff.

the contrary, what is expressed by πνεῦμα is rather the fact that man does not ever live by himself, or by what he possesses, but purely by the act of God, just as his δικαιοσύνη [1] is precisely the δικαιοσύνη θεοῦ. It is for this very reason that Paul can say that the ζωή that he now has is not his own, but that Christ lives in him (Gal. ii.19 f.; Rom. viii.10), that Christ's ζωή is in us (II Cor. iv.10 f.), or that we live in Christ (Rom. vi.11) and will live in him (II Cor. xiii.4) and that our life is in Christ (Rom. viii.2).[2] What is meant by that is not a 'Christ mysticism', but the fact that we have life only in relation to God's act of salvation in Christ.

(c) The concrete possibilities of life

In Stoicism, on the one hand, the existential moment is destroyed by being reduced to general terms; in Gnosticism, on the other, the concrete possibilities of life are neutralised by asceticism or indifference (cf. p. 26); but, for Paul, pneumatic ζωή is real ζωή precisely because it is effective at each particular moment in the real possibilities of life which the believer faces, remembering, however, the ὡς μή (I Cor. vii.29-31). It is freedom from death, because the believer has already made his own the death that is laid up for him in that he has died with Christ, because he has taken upon himself the cross, through which the world with its possibilities is crucified, and has thus, from this very death, gained life.[3] But this freedom from death (II Cor. iii.6-18 et al.) manifests

---

[1] cf. *Righteousness* (1951) in this series.

[2] The Pauline formula of the life in Christ is approached again in Ign. Eph. xi.1, xx.2; Pol. viii.1; his life in us Ign. Mg. v.2. The same is said in the Pauline concept of σῶμα χριστοῦ and this sense is followed by II Clem. when he speaks (xiv.1) of the ἐκκλησία τῆς ζωῆς, and (xiv.2) the ἐκκλησία ζῶσα is defined as σῶμα χριστοῦ.

[3] Gal. ii.19 f., vi.14; Rom. vi.1-11. Cf. pp. 93-99.

itself precisely in the believer's taking on himself, in service, the real possibilities of death and, thus in constantly dying, in his revealing the ζωή τοῦ Ἰησοῦ (II Cor. iv.8-16): . . . as dying and behold we live (II Cor. vi.4-10). The real possibilities of earthly life and death are swallowed up by Christ. Through life and death Paul glorifies only him and, as death is a κέρδος, so also the ζῆν ἐν σαρκί can only be καρπὸς ἔργου, i.e. a labour in the service of Christ (Phil. i.20-22).[1] Just as his ζωή is a life from God (or Christ), so also it is only for God (or Christ).[2] And so, naturally, life and death (as also waking and sleeping in I Thess. v.10) are made relative and indifferent matters, not, however, in the Stoic sense, but only because the believer belongs to Christ and God (I Cor. iii.22 f.), serves him (II Cor. v.9) and is inextricably bound up with God's ἀγάπη which was given in Christ (Rom. viii.38 f.). The result is that the real possibilities of existence are never directly, but only indirectly, through faith, the realities of his existence, yet at the same time this must be so as long as the believer does not see face to face. The ζῆν πνεύματι is a στοιχεῖν πνεύματι (Gal. v.25, cf. Rom. viii.12 ff.), whose first fruits is ἀγάπη (Gal. v.22 f.). Dying and rising again with Christ is a περιπατεῖν ἐν καινότητι ζωῆς(Rom. vi. 4), which is put into the imperative, and since it is the life that has come out of death, it must prove to be a way of life in righteousness (Rom. vi.12-23). Such a way of life, however, is not in itself ζωή in a notional sense, as is evident not only

---

[1] On Phil. i.21 see the commentaries. I cannot entirely agree with the explanation of O. Schmidt in *Neutestamentliche Studien fur Heinrici* (1914), pp. 155-169; τὸ ζῆν in verse 21 cannot be anything other that the ζωή in verse 20 and the ζῆν ἐν σαρκί of verse 22, that is the physical earthly life. This life means 'Christ' for him, i.e. it has found its meaning in Christ, for it has become pointless without him.

[2] Rom. vi.11, 13; Gal. ii.19 f; II Cor. v.15.

in that it is based on the previous gift of justification, but also in that ζωή, as an individual life, is not self-contained: for (i) ζωή is propagated in the word of preaching, i.e. the believer does not have ζωή for himself in the inwardness of a spiritual life, but, rather, he is placed in the strand of history which was started by the act of salvation and in which this ζωή is available for him who is obedient to the redemptive will (II Cor. ii.16, iv.12), and (ii) ζωή is never isolated in time, but, rather, the τέλος, the fruit of such a pneumatic life is itself ζωή (Rom. vi.22 f.; Gal. vi.8; Phil. iii.8-14). The old concept that only behaviour that agrees with God's will renders one worthy of αἰώνιος ζωή (cf. p. 62) is maintained, but it is given a new basis. Such behaviour itself grows first out of the ζωή that has already been given. It is because this basis is missing that the intention of fulfilling the will of God,[1] whose demands are found in the Law, leads to death. Thus, the ζωή of the believer is this very freedom from the νόμος [2] (II Cor. iii.17; Gal. v.1), a freedom which, because it is at the same time freedom from sin (Rom. vi.18, 22, viii.2), is a new subjection to the will of God (Rom. vi.2, 12-14, viii.2-10). By means of this dualism, which belongs to the concept of ζωή, the Pauline statement can vary in a peculiar way, in that (αἰώνιος) ζωή at one time denotes the future possession,[3] at another the present life (Rom. vi.4, 11, 13, viii.2-10) and often both are closely interwoven.[4] Paul did not seek to reconcile these concepts. A tentative approach may be found in the idea of a gradual transformation of the mortal body, as seems suggested in II Cor. iii.18,

---

[1] Which of course ought to lead to ζωή, Rom. vii.10, x.5; Gal. iii.12.   [2] cf. *Law* (1962) in the series.

[3] Rom. i.17, ii.7, v.17, 21, viii.13, 18-39; II Cor. v.1-10; Gal. vi.8.

[4] cf. Rom. vi, viii.2-10 and 11-13; II Cor. iv.7-16 and iv.17-v.10.

iv.16. Nevertheless such a transformation could never be understood as a natural process (indeed a 'natural' process of growth appears to Paul as miraculous in I Cor. xv.36-38). Paul always retained from the Jewish apocalyptic writings the idea of a miraculous transformation (I Cor. xv.51) in connection with a dramatic cosmic event (I Thess. iv.13-18; I Cor. xv) and, as the core of this eschatological hope, this at least has to be mentioned: not only has natural death become immaterial in the face of real ζωή given by God, but also the death that has already happened will one day be annulled by the resurrection and mortality will be finally abolished.[1]

(d) Future life

If it can be understood how real ζωή, as a thing of the present, is nevertheless 'other-worldly', as a thing of the future it is, of course, beyond the grasp of any imagination. If it can be described negatively in the traditional terminology as a σωθῆναι,[2] then it can also be described positively, and also traditionally, as δόξα.[3] If, for this life in δόξα, the possibilities of earthly life disappear (Rom. xiv.17), it is nevertheless considered that a bodiless life is unimaginable for Paul.[4] At the same time any precise description and especially any thought of the incorporation of the soul into the ranks of the cosmic powers is absent. Only hints are given: δικαιοσύνη καὶ εἰρήνη καὶ χαρὰ ἐν πνεύματι ἁγίω (Rom. xiv.17); a βλέπειν πρόσωπον πρὸς πρόσωπον

---

[1] I Cor. xv.23-26, 50-57; II Cor. v.1-5; Phil. iii.20 f.

[2] Rom. v.10. Cf. σωτηρία as the aim of faith, Rom. i.16 f.; x.9 f., etc.

[3] cf. especially II Cor. iii.6-11 where the elevation of the new διακονία over the old one is described by the contrasts between θάνατος—πνεῦμαζωοποιοῦν: κατάκρισις—δικαιοσύνη: τὸ καταργούμενον—τὸ μένον.

[4] I Cor. xv.35-54; II Cor. v.1-5; Phil. iii.21.

(I Cor. xiii.12, cf. II Cor. v.7); a complete knowledge; the abiding of πίστις, ἐλπίς, ἀγάπη; being with or near Christ.[1]

6. *Life as present reality according to John*

(a) *Life and the revealer*

Ζωή is represented as a thing of the present still more radically in John. That is connected with the fact that he already traces the resurrection of Jesus to the fact that Jesus, as the λόγος of God and the eternal Son of God, is life and has life within himself,[2] and that, too, as a divine creative power, not merely as the power of being alive as a living being. As such he naturally has a ψυχή and gives it up to death (x.11, 15, 17), whilst his ζωή is not interrupted by death.[3] His ζωή is already described as the φῶς τῶν ἀνθρώπων before the incarnation (i.4), because it was in the dependence of the whole creation on him that there lay for men the possibility of possessing life in him as the revelation of God, by turning back in understanding to their source. If he is described as ζωή, it is not as a cosmic force which could be grasped by speculation, but, rather, as the revealer of God, for whom himself, by fulfilling God's commission to reveal, the ἐντολή of God is ζωὴ αἰώνιος (xii.50) and who, as revealer, gives faith the possibility of real life. It is in this sense that he calls himself the ζωή (xi.25, xiv.6) or describes himself as the ἄρτος τῆς ζωῆς (vi.35, 48),[4] as the φῶς τῆς ζωῆς (viii.12), as the one who gives the ὕδωρ ζῶν (iv.10 f., vii.38) and the ἄρτος ζῶν (vi.50 f.), i.e. precisely as the revealer. His

---

[1] I Thess. iv.17; II Cor. v.8; Phil. i.23.

[2] John i.4, v.26, vi.57; I John i.1 f.; v.11, 20.

[3] cf. in John xiv.19 the present: ὅτι ἐγὼ ζῶ with the contrast καὶ ὑμεῖς ζήσεσθε.

[4] See E. Janot, 'Le Pain de Vie', *Gregorianum* XI (1930), pp. 161-170.

words are πνεῦμα καὶ ζωή (vi.63), or ῥήματα ζωῆς αἰωνίου (vi.68). In addition he has come to give life to the world (vi.33, x.10; I John iv.9).

(b) The presence of life in faith

However, since, as the revealer, he is and gives ζωή (I John i.1 f.), and since it was with his coming that ζωή was revealed, believers already have ζωή as a present fact in faith.[1] The paradoxical nature of this assertion is expressly stressed: whoever believes has already passed from death into life (v.24; I John iii.14); now, as he is speaking (and for the evangelist that also means every occasion when the Word is proclaimed) the eschatological hour takes place (v.25). He is, as the speaker, the ἀνάστασις and the ζωή, so that whoever believes in him lives, though he might die; indeed, in the true sense, he will not die at all (xi.25). He has already given the δόξα to his own in the revelation (xvii.22). Correspondingly, the promises relating to the future do not refer to a later eschatological future, but to the moment of decision when confronted with the Word. Whoever believes shall live.[2] Yet, at the same time, this ζωή is not understood in the timeless, idealist sense. It is a ζωή that has an everlasting future (iv.14, vi.27, xii.25), and his own people, to whom he has given his δόξα, are nevertheless directed to the future vision of δόξα in fellowship with the glorified Son (xvii.24).

However, in the Gospel explicit allusions to an eschatological future in the sense of the Jewish and primitive Christian eschatology, which Paul still retained, are entirely absent except for v.28 f. (future ἀνάστασις) and vi.51b-56 (the partaking of the Lord's

---

[1] John iii.15 f., 36; vi.40, 47, xx.31; I John iii.15; v.11, 13.
[2] John iv.14, v.25, vi.51, 58, xiv.19; I John iv.9 and the ἵνα clauses such as John v.40, vi.40.

Supper as a guarantee of ἀνάστασις at the ἐσχάτη ἡμέρα; and also the additions concerning the ἐσχάτη ἡμέρα in vi.39, 40, 44, xii.48). If it is considered impossible to interpret the latter passages in the light of the former and just as impossible to reconcile both into a homogeneous view, the statements just listed will be attributed to an editing of the Gospel which strives after a compromise with the traditional eschatology, as is also done in I John ii.28 f., iii.2, iv.17.

(c) The presence of life in love and joy

The essential thing, at any rate, is to understand the present nature of ζωή. Just as it is not an ideal entity, so also it does not consist of an inward spiritual life, as, for example, in a mystic sense. For John did not spiritualise the primitive Christian eschatology and thereby dissolve it, but, rather, in the same tradition as Jesus and Paul, radicalised it. That is, he took seriously the idea that the coming of Jesus as the revealer is the decisive eschatological event, the κρίσις.[1] It is not in relation to an idea or a suprahistorical, metaphysical being, but by adhering in faith to an historical fact and an historical person that ζωή is attained, and, correspondingly, this life consists in the manner of an historical existence, in the certainty that comes through the word of revelation, which teaches one to understand any given moment in a new way, free from the past and open to the future. Life is at the same time the way and the objective. In the last discourses, as in I John, this is made plain in that the life of the believer is shown to stand under the ἐντολή, the ἐντολή of ἀγάπη. For abiding in him (xv.1-8) is abiding in love (xv.9-17). That just such conduct is life follows from the fact that

---

[1] John iii.18 f., v.27, xii.31; cf. xii.46-48 and the μένειν of the ὀργή iii.36 and of the ἁμαρτία ix.41. R. Bultmann, *Zwischen den Zeiten* 6 (1928), pp. 4-22.

that act of loving is after all based on having been loved (xiii.34, xv.12; I John iv.7-10) and is therefore, together with faith, the receiving of revelation; i.e. is life. For that reason love for the brethren is the criterion for the μεταβεβηκέναι ἐκ τοῦ θανάτου εἰς τὴν ζωήν (I John iii.14 f.). If ζωή, so to speak, manifests itself outwardly in ἀγάπη, it does so inwardly in παρρησία (I John iii.21, v.14), in which φόβος is overcome (I John iv.18) and in which joy in prayer consists,[1] and does so in χαρά,[2] in which all λύπη is overcome (xvi.20-22). But all this is not as a διάθεσις of the soul, but in its relationship to revelation, in which clarity (παρρησία) is present; a clarity in the face of which every question and every puzzle vanishes (xvi.23, 25, 29). Thus ζωή can be defined as knowledge of God and of the one whom he sent (xvii.3). Whoever has this ζωή has everything (x.10; ἵνα ζωὴν καὶ περισσὸν ἔχωσιν).

(d) The relationship with the Hellenistic concept of life

In such a view John comes close to the view of Hellenistic philosophy of religion and mythology and moves within its terminology.[3] Yet it would be misunderstanding the religio-historical relationship if one were to speak simply of dependence for, in fact, a completely different outlook is present. Just as John treats radically the Judaeo-Christian view of life and the eschatology connected with it, so also, in a certain sense, he treats the popular Hellenistic and the Gnostic view of life. If with him ζωή and φῶς characterise the revelation, it is hardly without conscious antithesis to

---

[1] John xiv.13 f., xv.7, 16, xvi.23 f.; I John v.15.
[2] John xv.11, xvi.20-24, xvii.13; I John i.4.
[3] In this sense I must agree with the concept of John as it is given (e.g.) in W. Bousset, *Kyrios Christos* ([2]1921) and in W. Bauer, *Kommentar zum Johannesevangelium* ([3]1933) as against Fr. Büchsel, *Johannes und der hellenistische Syncretismus* (1928).

Gnosticism, yet it is not a simple polemical contrast. For if he takes over the scheme of the Gnostic redemption myth for his Christology,[1] he is thereby saying that he recognises the question that was alive for Gnosticism, that of ζωή, as a question, that he is transforming it and providing the answer. That is also evident in his interpretation of the concepts ἀλήθεια [2] and γνῶσις.[3] Even if one cannot point to direct literary connections with semimythological speculation and speculation that half bears the mark of the Hellenistic philosophy of religion, nevertheless the historical connections with ideas such as were formulated later in Plotinus and in the Hellenistic writings and at an earlier date in Philo are unquestionable. The sentence about ζωή as the knowledge of God and of Jesus Christ (xvii.3) is to be understood as the antithesis to them; i.e. the man desiring ζωή is led from speculation and mysticism to revelation.[4] Thus the statements receive their full force with the ἐγώ εἰμι: what is sought for everywhere is here made real. That does not mean that those questions are merely false. They have a positive value. From this comes the full meaning of i.4 also: ἡ ζωὴ ἦν τὸ φῶς τῶν ἀνθρώπων, where the characteristic of light belonging to the ζωή of creation is described not as a finished past fact, but as a fact of the present, even if the κόσμος has shut its eyes to the φῶς of this ζωή (i.5). The φῶς of the λόγος is effective also in the σκοτία, because in the σκοτία the question of ζωή is a vital one. For σκοτία is only what it is in contrast with the φῶς, and the idea that everything only has its being through the λόγος is not annulled. The question,

---

[1] cf. W. Bauer, *Op. cit.*; R. Bultmann, ZNW 24 (1925), pp. 100-146; H. Odeberg, *The Fourth Gospel*, I (1929).

[2] cf. TWNT I, p. 245.

[3] cf. *Gnosis* (1952) in this series, p. 48.

[4] cf. the quotation of John v.24 in Plotinus *Enn.* I 4, 4.

of course, may be deceptively posed and may suggest that life is to be found where none exists (v.39 f.). But the question, the ἐρευνᾶν, exists and appears in that the κόσμος has the idea of ζωή at all. Revelation, therefore, links up with this concept in order to lead men from the false to the real ζωή. John has given expression to this positive meaning of the concepts that were alive in the κόσμος (and therefore, historically speaking, in Gnostic piety) in that he describes the revelation as ὕδωρ ζῶν or ἄρτος ζῶν (τῆς ζωῆς). In doing this he forges a link with the widespread desire for and the fables of a water of life and of a food of life. All hunger and thirst does not in actual fact demand instantaneous satisfaction and, basically, does not desire some particular thing, but what does make itself felt is a seeking after and a desire for life itself. Everything that is not genuine and real points with a question mark, to what is genuine and real. For that reason both the Samaritan woman and the 'Jews' understand Jesus in a way when he offers ὕδωρ ζῶν and ἄρτος ζῶν and they ask for it.[1]

[1] Later, in the Alexandrians, the Johannine terminology, with its original Gnostic sense, is almost completely modified again by the influence of Gnostic thinking. But the terminology of Ignatius, which is related to that of John, shows rather the sphere from which John has taken his understanding, the sphere of mythological sacramental thinking. For Ignatius Jesus Christ is ἐν θανάτῳ ζωὴ ἀληθινή: Eph. vii.2. He is revealed εἰς καινότητα ἀϊδίου ζωῆς: Eph. xix.3. Through his participation in the sacraments Ignatius can say: ὕδωρ δὲ ζῶν καὶ λαλοῦν ἐν ἐμοί: Rom. vii.2. So after the manner of this Gnostic thinking, Ignatius modifies the Pauline usage under the influence of which he stands (p. 66, n. 1). Gnostic-Johannine concepts of deliverance (ἰατρός; νοῦς; φῶς; ζωή) Dg. ix.6 are transferred as formulae referring to God. The combination of ζωή and γνῶσις (Dg. xii.2-7) has also become formal.

ADDITIONAL NOTE TO CHAPTER IV

1. ἀναζάω

ἀναζῆν, to come to life again, to revive, a late word, little attested.[1] It appears neither in the LXX nor elsewhere in Jewish-Hellenistic literature.[2] It is used of the coming to life again of the dead in Rev. xx.5 (ἀνέζησαν as a variant reading for ἔζησαν) and of Christ's resurrection in Rom. xiv.9 (as a variant reading with ἀνέστη for ἔζησεν). In the same sense, but figuratively, in Luke xv.24: οὗτος ὁ υἱός μου νεκρὸς ἦν καὶ ἀνέζησεν (variant reading ἔζησεν, this is the reading better attested in verse 32 together with ἀνέζησεν). In Rom. vii.9, without the ἀνα-('again') being stressed, it says (χωρὶς γὰρ νόμου ἡ ἁμαρτία νεκρά . . .) ἐλθούσης δὲ τῆς ἐντολῆς ἡ ἁμαρτιὰ ἀνέζησεν, ἐγὼ δὲ ἀπέθανον. The word is not used by the Apostolic Fathers and the apologists.

2. Ζῷον

In Greek ζῷον means living creature, it is used of human beings and animals, the latter, as the ἄλογα ζῷα, being distinguished from the former, as the λογικὰ ζῷα (the Stoic term). Nevertheless in common usage ζῷον means for the most part simply 'animal', as it is in the LXX: Gen. i.21; Ps. lxviii.11 [LXX lxvii.11]; civ.25 [LXX ciii.25]; Ezek.xlvii.9 (for ḥayyā); Wisd. vii.20,

---

[1] T. Nägeli, Der Wortschatz des Apostels Paulus (1905), p. 47. J. A. Deissmann, Licht vom Osten (⁴1923). Conforming with the Attic ζῶ—ἐβίων, ἀναζῶ—ἀναβιῶν could have been expected. But to live again is a typical aorist form. The present gradually to come alive again is not usual and is therefore hardly found. The perfect ἀναβιώσκεσθαι occurs instead. Instead of ἀναβιῶναι (ἀναβιῶσαι) we find the Ionian-Hellenistic form ἀναζῆσαι.

[2] LXX (F²) reads in Gen. xlv.27: ἀνάζησεν τὸ πνεῦμα Ἰακώβ. Josephus uses both ἀναβιοῦν and ἀναβιῶσαι. See p. 48, n. 1.

xi.15 *et al.* In the New Testament: Heb. xiii.11.[1] Only where the animal level to which teachers of heretical doctrine have sunk is expressly emphasised does it say ἄλογα ζῷα (Jude 10; II Peter ii.12).[2] Just as in Ezek. i.5, 13 ff., etc., the wonderful heavenly creatures, the cherubim, are described as ζῷα (*ḥayyōt*), so in Rev. iv.6 ff.; v.6 ff., etc., the four creatures round God's throne are also described. This corresponds to the usage found in inscriptions and on papyri, which describes the miraculous divine animals of the Egyptians as ζῷα.[3] So also the wonderful bird, the Phoenix is called ζῷον in I Clem. xxv.3. Human beings and animals are comprehended together as ζῷα in I Clem. xx.4.[4]

3. *Ζωογονέω*

Ζωογονεῖν,[5] in Greek, is used since the time of Aristotle and Theophrastus to mean *to vivify, to bring forth* and, moreover, almost only of the φύσις of animals and plants and very seldom of human beings.[6] Nature's power of bringing forth life is sometimes traced back to the deity.[7]

---

[1] Also I Clem. xx.4, 10, xxxiii.3; Barn. x.7 f. Often in the Apologists, e.g. Just. *Apol.* lv.4; *Dial.* iii.6, iv.4.

[2] Also Just. *Apol.* xxiv.1, lv.4; *Dial.* cvii.2 *et al.* λογικὸν ζῷον occurs in Just. *Dial.* xciii.3.

[3] cf. F. Preisigke, *Wörterbuch der griechischen Papyrusurkunden* (1925 ff.), and Pr.-Bauer on Athenag. Suppl. 18.3. For ζῷα in Revelation, cf. the commentaries and H. Gunkel, *Zum religionsgeschichtlichen Verständnis des NT* (²1910), pp. 43-47, and F. Boll, *Aus der Offenbarung Johannes* (1914), pp. 36-38.

[4] Naturally the apologists are familiar with this usage, e.g. Just. *Dial.* iii.7, iv.2, cvii.2.

[5] More likely ζωογονεῖν (from ζωός, ζῶς) meaning *to create life*, than ζῳογονεῖν meaning *to create living beings* (ζῷα).

[6] Theophr. *De Causis Plantarum* IV. 15.4 (ζωογονεῖσθαι of 'to plant'): Athenaeus VII.52 (p. 298c) (ζωογονεισθαι of the seed of the eel in the mud): Lucian *Dialogi Deorum* 8 (παρθένον ζωογονῶν of Zeus). [7] cf. e.g. Lucian *Amores* 19.

In the LXX ζωογονεῖν more than once renders the
pi'el and hiph'il of *ḥyh*. Animals (*haḥayyā*) are
called τὰ ζωογονοῦντα in Lev. xi.47. It says of God
in I Sam. ii.6: κύριος θανατοῖ καὶ ζωογονεῖ.[1] Differing
from the Greek usage,[2] ζωογονεῖν is more than once
used to mean *to let someone live* (the subject of the verb
always being human beings, the opposite always being
to kill): Exod. i.17 f., 22; Judges viii.19; I Sam. xxvii.9,
11; I Kings xx [LXX xxi]. 31; II Kings vii.4.
In the New Testament ζωογονεῖν is found as a
predicate of God in I Tim. vi.13 just as in Greek:
τοῦ θεοῦ τοῦ ζωογονοῦντος (ζωοποιοῦντος variant reading)
τὰ πάντα. Ζωογονεῖν is not used in the specifically
Christian (soteriological) sense as distinct from ζωοποιεῖν
(see below). On the other hand it is used in the non-
classical sense of the LXX in Acts vii.19 (following
Exod. i.17 f.) and Luke xvii.33: ὃς ἂν ἀπολέσει
(τὴν ψυχὴν) ζωογονήσει αὐτήν.[3]
Ζωογονεῖν is absent in the Apostolic fathers. It
occurs once in the Apologists: Tatian, *Oratio ad Graecos*
12.2.

4. Ζωοποιέω

ζωοποιεῖν, as ζωογονεῖν, is used in Greek since
Aristotle and Theophrastus to mean *to vivify*, usually
of the generation of animals or (in the middle voice)

---

[1] Instead of this II Kings v.7: ζωοποιεῖν, Deut. xxxii.39:
ζῆν ποιεῖν.

[2] At least one can show this in Diod. S. 23.4 where ζωογονεῖσθαι
is used of the growing up, 'the surviving', of the children of
Semele.

[3] This is not good Greek (against A. Schlatter, *Lukasevangelium*
(1911), p. 555), being only found in the LXX. In parallels
περιποιεῖσθαι stands, which occasionally renders the pi'el of ḥāyāh
in the LXX (Gen. xii.12; Exod. xxii.18), also in the variant
reading of Mark viii.35. Σῴζειν is used which can render the
pi'el (Ps. xxx.3 [LXX xxix.4]) and the hiph'il (Gen. xlvii.25).

of the growing of plants. In this sense ζωοποιεῖν is also predicable of the deity.[1] The LXX uses ζωοποιεῖν to render the pi'el and hiph'il of *ḥyh*. Here God is almost without exception the subject of ζωοποιεῖν.[2] The usage here is nowhere unclassical and yet life (with God seen as its creator) is not primarily the life of nature, but the salvation of the people and of the godly (cf. p. 17). On the other hand, in Judges xxi.14 and Job xxxvi.6 ζωοποιεῖν is used, like ζωογονεῖν, in the sense to let someone live (the opposite of to kill).

In the New Testament and in the Apostolic Fathers ζωοποιεῖν is used without exception to mean to vivify in the soteriological sense. The subject is naturally God or Christ or also the πνεῦμα.[3] It is expressly said of the Law that it cannot make alive (Gal. iii.21). Just as God in Rom. iv.17 is described as ζωοποιῶν τοὺς νεκροὺς καὶ καλῶν τὰ μὴ ὄντα ὡς ὄντα, so also ζωοποιοῦν by itself is used of the eschatological resurrection of the dead: Rom. viii.11: ὁ ἐγείρας ἐκ νεκρῶν χριστὸν Ἰησοῦν ζωοποιήσει καὶ τὰ θνητὰ σώματα ὑμῶν; likewise in I Cor. xv.22: ὥσπερ γὰρ ἐν τῷ Ἀδὰμ πάντες ἀποθνῃσκουσιν, οὕτως καὶ ἐν τῷ χριστῷ πάντες ζωοποιηθήσονται.[4] ζωοποιεῖν is, therefore, synonymous with ἐγείρειν (cf. II Cor. i.9 with Rom. iv.17), in the same way that in John v.21 (as in Rom. viii.11) both words appear side by side: ὥσπερ γὰρ ὁ πατὴρ ἐγείρει τοὺς νεκροὺς καὶ ζωοποιεῖ, οὕτως καὶ ὁ υἱὸς οὓς θέλει ζωοποιεῖ. In the same sense ζωοποιεῖν is applied to the resurrection of Christ in I Peter iii.18: θανατωθεὶς μὲν

---

[1] cf. e.g. *Corp. Herm.* IX.6, XI.17, XII.22, XVI.8.
[2] cf. II Kings v.7; Ps. lxxi (LXX lxx) 20; II Esdr. ix.8 f.; Eccles. vii.13. Cf. Letter of Aristeas 16.
[3] Once of the baptismal water in Herm. s. IX. 16.2, 7.
[4] Also Barn. vi.17, vii.2, xii.5, 7 (Christ or his πληγή as subject).

σαρκί, ζωοποιηθεὶς δὲ πνεύματι.[1] Just as the eschatological ζωή is, in a certain sense, a thing of the present (cf. p. 65), so also the divine ζωοποιεῖν can refer to the present. This is so in John v.21, also in Col. ii.13; Eph. ii.5 and where there is mention of the ζωοποιεῖν of the πνεῦμα: I Cor. xv.45; II Cor. iii.3; John vi.63.[2] In the same sense it is said of the Christians in Dg. v.12: θανατοῦνται καὶ ζωοποιοῦνται; and again v.16: κολαζόμενοι χαίρουσιν ὡς ζωοποιούμενοι.[3]

---

[1] Therefore the NT can say συζωοποιεῖν of the resurrection of Christ which is the reason for the resurrection of the faithful. (This word is not attested earlier, nor does it occur in the Apostolic Fathers or the Apologists.) Col. ii.13: ὑμᾶς νεκροὺς ὄντας τοῖς παραπτώμασιν . . . συνεζωοποίησεν σὺν αὐτῷ, χαρισάμενος ἡμῖν πάντα τὰ παραπτώματα . . .); Eph. ii.5.

[2] See J. Sickenberger, Die Briefe des heiligen Paulus and die Römer und Korinther (⁴1932), p. 80.

[3] In the Greek usage ζωοποιεῖσθαι is said of the seed in I Cor. xv.36. Also in this sense but used metaphorically in Herm. m. IV.3.7.

V. DEATH IN THE NEW TESTAMENT

1. New Testament Usage

In the NT ἀποθνῄσκειν (perfect τέθνηκα without ἀπο) and τελευτᾶν describe primarily and most frequently the act of dying (present: *to be dying*; aorist: *to die* (simply); perfect: *to be dead*). θάνατος (once τελευτή in Matt. ii.15) [1] is the process of dying (e.g. Heb. vii.23) as also the state of being dead (e.g. Phil. i.20). Death is the universal fate of man, [2] while death is alien only to God and the eternal world (I Tim. vi.16;

[1] For *dying* the NT also uses κοιμᾶσθαι, e.g. John xi.11; Acts vii.60, xiii.36; I Cor. vii.39, etc. (so too the Apostolic Fathers) see Pr.-Bauer. Correspondingly οἱ κοιμώμενοι (I Thess. iv.13) or οἱ κεκοιμημένοι (I Cor. xv.20) are *those who have fallen asleep*. Κοιμᾶσθαι has been used in Greek since Homer for the sleep of death, also on inscriptions and in papyri (see Liddell and Scott, Pr.-Bauer sv., L. Radermacher *Neutestamentliche Grammatik* (²1925), p. 108). It is met in the LXX for *šākab* (*to lie*, or *lie down*), e.g. Gen. xlvii.30; II Sam. vii.12; I Kings ii.10. The Rabbis talk likewise of *falling asleep* (usually *dᵉmak*, see Str.-B. I, p. 1040 on Matt. xxvii.53. Schlatter, *Matthäusevangelium*, p. 784, *Johannesevangelium*, p. 249, or *those who have fallen asleep* Str.-B. III, p. 634). The noun κοίμησις, which in John xi.13 is used in a double sense, as the κοίμησις τοῦ ὕπνου and of the death, also means sleep of death in Greek (A. Audollent, *Defixionum Tabellae* (1914), 242, 30, etc. R. Wunsch, *Antike Fluchtafeln* KlT 20 (1907), pp. 4, 30). Also in LXX Ecclus. xlvi.19, xlviii.13; on Romano-Jewish tombs and in Herm. v. III. 11.3, s. IX.15.6 (Pr.-Bauer). Cf. also M. Lidzbarski, *Das Johannesbuch der Mandäer* (1915), p. 168, 6 f.

[2] John vi.49, 58; viii.52 f., Heb. vii.8, ix.27. We are slaves to death, Barn. xvi.9. Exceptions: Enoch, Heb. xi.5, and Melchizedek, Heb. vii.3, 16 f. The human σῶμα is θνητόν: Rom. vi.12, viii.11; I Cor. xv.53 f.; cf. II Cor. iv.11, v.4; I Clem. xxxix.2: τί γὰρ δύναται θνητός ἢ τις ἰσχὺς γηγενοῦς. Death can be used in connection with both animals (Matt. viii.32 *et al.*) and plants (John xii.24; I Cor. xv.36; differently Jude 12).

I Cor. xv.53). It is a source of terror [1] which is feared [2] and which is looked for only under the most terrible circumstances (Rev. ix.6). Dying is nowhere glorified and even if Paul knows of heroic death for others and puts Christ's death in a certain analogy to it (Rom. v.7), Christ's death is nevertheless not understood as an heroic achievement (cf. p. 93). Nor is the sacrifice of death, which in certain circumstances, the apostle makes for others (II Cor. iv.12), nor the steadfastness of the martyr to the point of death (Rev. ii.10, xii.11). For there is never the idea that the one who sacrifices himself neutralises death for his own person. It is characteristic that suicide is never made a problem.[3] On the contrary death always remains a source of terror which makes ζωή an unreal ζωή (cf. p. 60).[4] The work of Christ consists precisely in the fact that he has destroyed death (II Tim. i.10; cf. p. 96). Death is the ἔσχατος ἐχθρός with whose ultimate destruction the process of salvation has reached its end (I Cor. xv.26; Rev. xx.14).

The attempt is nowhere made to interpret death as a natural occurrence and thus to neutralise it. Even where its abolition through resurrection is thought of and dying and rising again are described according to the analogy of a natural process (I Cor. xv.36; John xii.24), it is not conceived of as a natural occurrence any more than the resurrection. That event, used as an

---

[1] Rev. vi.8, xviii.8; Herm. s. VI.2.4.: ὁ δὲ θάνατος ἀπώλειαν ἔχει αἰώνιον. Old expressions appear again such as *a sickness unto death* (Phil. ii.27, 30; John xi.4; cf. Rev. xiii.3, 12) *sorrowful unto death* (Mark xiv.34 and parallels), *persecution unto death* (Acts xxii.4; I Clem. iv.9; cf. v.2). Death can also be given as an earthly punishment (Mark x.33 *et al.*). θάνατος as the danger of death, II Cor. i.10, xi.23.   [2] Heb. ii.15; cf. Rom. viii.15.

[3] On Augustine's criticism of the Stoic idea of suicide, cf. E. Benz, *Das Todesproblem in der Stoischen Philosophie* (1929), pp. 119 ff.

[4] In Ign. Sm. v.1 the contrasting of θάνατος and ἀλήθεια.

analogy, is not in the biblical sense to be understood
as a natural process in the Greek scientific sense. The
origin and reason for it can, it is true, be understood
mythologically, where death is thought of as a demonic
person (I Cor. xv.26; Rev. vi.8, xx.13 f.), or where
the lord of death is said to be the devil (Heb. ii.14;
cf. p. 44). In such mythological passages,[1] however,
which in any case do not serve any aetiological purpose,
the idea is expressed that death is opposed to life which
is the intrinsic nature of God (cf. p. 60) and consequently death and sin belong together.

2. Death as the result of and the punishment for sin [2]

The question of the origin of death is, therefore,
bound to become the question of the origin of sin.
This question also, where it is dealt with, corresponding
to the understanding of ἁμαρτία, is not dealt with
in a speculative way.

A few statements of Paul, in which he takes over the
Gnostic 'Anthropos-myth', do it is true touch on the
speculative in passing (cf. p. 67). Where he conceives
Adam and Christ as prototypes, who each institute and
determine the nature of a human race, he goes beyond
the Jewish idea of Adam, and death (and sin) (cf. pp.

[1] II Cor. xi.3 has an allusion to the myths, cf. H. Lietzmann
and H. Windisch, Commentaries ad loc. It is significant that in
Rom. v.12 ff. every reference to the mythological figures of death
and the devil is omitted.

[2] This conviction is the same in both the NT and in Judaism; see
pp. 43 f. References: Rom. i.32, vi.16, 21, 23, vii.5: καρποφορῆσαι
τῷ θανάτῳ viii.6, 13; I Cor. xv.56: τὸ δὲ κέντρον τοῦ θανάτου ἡ
ἁμαρτία; James i.15: ἡ δὲ ἁμαρτία ἀποτελεσθεῖσα ἀποκυεῖ θάνατον;
cf. Gal. vi.7 f.; II Cor. vii.10; John viii.21, 24; I John v.16 f.; Barn.
xii.2, 5; I Clem. iii.4; II Clem. i.6; Herm. v. II.3.1; m. II.1;
XII.6.2; s. VIII.8.5; VIII.11.3 et al. Particular sins are said to be
παγὶς θανάτου: Did. ii.4; Barn. xix.7 f. The same picture in the
OT: Prov. xiv.27, xxi.6, etc.

43 f.) and life appear as cosmic forces. At the same time, in Rom. v.12 ff., the speculative element has moved away in so far as sin is seen completely as an act which has to be answered for with death as its consequences. I Cor. xv. 21 f. will have to be interpreted in this sense; but the tone of I Cor. xv.44-49 implies that Adamic man was created from the first as subject to death; Adam only became a ψυχὴ ζῶσα, while Christ became πνεῦμα ζωοποιοῦν, the former was ἐκ γῆς χοϊκός, the latter ἐξ οὐρανοῦ ἐπουράνιος. If Paul really means that, the result would be that he distinguishes death proper from mere mortality which has not acquired the character of θάνατος. That is nowhere expressly stated, it is true, but Paul does say that death came into this world through Adam (I Cor. xv.22), that is through Adam's sin (Rom. v.12, 17 f.).[1] Speculative questioning is not satisfied by this because Paul does not mean to exonerate the individual by this sentence: for each person death is the punishment for his own sin.[2] Even if Paul in Rom. v.14 (which is at least in formal contradiction to Rom. i.18 ff.) speaks as if the people in the period from Adam to Moses were indeed responsible for their own death as a result of their own sin (but not for their ἁμαρτάνειν which ensued in the Adamic succession since they did not violate any express command), then a twofold fact emerges: (i) Paul does not trace sin back to something that is not exactly sin, such as matter, sensuality or the like, but says sin came into the world through sin; (ii) in his preaching Paul only has people

---

[1] The idea of the guilt of Eve, which is met in Judaism (cf. p. 44, n. 1), is alluded to in II Cor. xi.3, I Tim. ii.14, but is found explicitly in Barn. xii.5.

[2] ἐφ' ᾧ πάντες ἥμαρτον: Rom. v.12 must have this sense. Moreover see p. 87, n. 2 and especially Rom. v.12-21, cf. J. Freundorfer, Erbsünde und Erbtod (Nt. liche Abhandlungen XIII 1/2 (1927), pp. 216 ff.).

in mind who are responsible for their own sin and thus for their death. The speculative ideas that are used in Rom. v and I Cor. xv serve to make clear the inescapability of sin and death for man, and Christ as the only means of salvation. They do not serve to take away the responsibility of man but show that, even with his responsibility, he cannot justify himself before God.[1]

That is shown also by the second answer Paul gives to the question of the origin of death. If sin is the κέντρον τοῦ θανάτου then at the same time it also holds true ἡ δὲ δύναμις τῆς ἁμαρτίας ὁ νόμος (I Cor. xv.56). It is the Law in practice that effects death. The letter of the Law kills (II Cor. iii.6) so that the office of the Law is called διακονία τοῦ θανάτου (II Cor. iii.7, verse 9: διακονία τῆς κατακρίσεως). Just as the disobedience of Adam to God's command brought about death (Rom. v.12 ff.) and as the Gentiles incurred the anger of God, which brought death, because they knew his demand for justice (δικαίωμα Rom. i.32) and violated it, so also for the Jewish people after Moses the idea is that the Law brought death because through it the sin which was dormant in man was awakened (Rom. vii.5, 10, 13). Without a doubt Paul's intention here is to assert the responsibility of man and the punitive character of death without allowing liberation from death to appear as a human possibility.

For this reason he traces sin, which brings death in its trail, back to σάρξ which characterises the real essence of man. Σάρξ is not, however, as used by Gnosticism, base matter in which the soul of man is imprisoned nor a demonic force to which man is subjected without responsibility, but rather man himself in his guilty, lost state, that is, man himself in so far as he regards himself from the sphere of σάρξ, i.e. from what is visible, verifiable (Rom. ii.28 f.; II Cor. iv.18) whether

[1] cf. Sin (1951) in this series.

natural data, historical conditions or tangible accomplishments.[1] Since all that is transient, under the sway of death, then that man is also under the sway of death from the start who wishes to gain his life from this point of departure. However, that is the way of the man who wants to live for himself instead of for God. He can live in absolutely no other way than for the σάρξ. The link between flesh, sin and death is thus established and thereby also that between Law and death. For as every striving of man to get free from death by himself and to earn life by achievements is itself only a desire to live in his own strength, it entangles him still further in sin and death, so that even the Law, which should lead to life, in fact leads to death (Rom. vii.10). He cannot free himself by himself.[2]

Not in explicit argument, as in Paul's letters, but implicitly John says the same, namely that outside the revelation in Jesus mankind is under the sway of death and that it is responsible for this because it is sinful. Its sin is nothing less than that it will not see itself from the creator's point of view as a creature (John i.4 f., cf. p. 74) but regards itself from its own point of view, as is shown in that it believes it has, over against God, its own criteria in the light of which his revelation must be proved (v.31 ff., viii.13 ff.). It is shown in that mankind believes itself to be free (viii.33) and that instead of seeking God's glory it set up its own standards of glory (v.41 ff.). So man is in sin and death (viii.21-24, 34-47).

3. *Death as inescapable*

The N.T. statements are not in complete agreement as to how far the essential nature of death lies in that

---

[1] cf. R. Bultmann, RGG[2] IV. 1034 f.

[2] Rom. vii.24. Cf. R. Bultmann in *Imago Dei, Festschrift für G. Krüger* (1932), pp. 53-62.

it destroys or how far in that it leads to torment beyond death. To some extent the traditional Jewish ideas of the punishment of Hell are prevalent (Mark ix.48; Luke xvi.23 *et al.*). In any case it is always maintained that God or Christ is the κριτὴς ζώντων καὶ νεκρῶν (cf. p. 59), that bodily death is not the absolute end but that it is followed by judgement (Heb. ix.27) and consequently that bodily death is annulled by the resurrection, or, where only the resurrection of the righteous is expected, that death is followed by a period of torment in hell.[1] Paul could not have expected a resurrection of the righteous only, even if I Cor. xv.22-24 and I Thess. iv.15 ff. can be understood in this way. Rom. ii.5-13, 16; II Cor. v.10 contradict it. Concerning the intermediate state between death and resurrection the N.T. contains no explicit statements. It might be thought of as sleep (cf. p. 85, n. 1) if many authors did not take other ideas for granted. In any case through the judgement of God bodily death becomes irrevocable death. For this reason there can be occasionally mention of the δεύτερος θάνατος (Rev. ii.11, xx.6, 14, xxi.8).[2] It is the torment of Hell that is thought of here (Rev. xxi.8: ἐν τῇ λίμνῃ

---

[1] As in Judaism (cf. p. 45) the ideas vary as to whether there is a general or partial resurrection. The latter in Luke xiv.14, cf. H. Molitor, *Die Auferstehung der Christen und Nichtchristen nach dem Apostel Paulus* (*Neutestamentliche Abhandlungen* XVI 1(1933), pp. 53 ff.).

[2] But for the idea of the second death in Judaism see p. 45, n. 2. Possibly Egyptian ideas have had some influence. G. Roeder, *Urkunden zur Religion des Alten Ägypten* (1923), indexed under 'to die' and 'death'. F. Boll, *Aus der Offenbarung Johannes* (1914), p. 49, n. 1. Frequently in the Mandaean writings, cf. M. Lidzbarski, *Ginza* (1925), index. According to Oecumenius, *Commentary on Revelation*, p. 221 (ed. H. C. Hoskier, 1928) the πρῶτος θάνατος is: ὁ αἰσθητός, ὁ χωρισμὸν ἔχων ψυχῆς καὶ σώματος, δεύτερος δὲ ὁ νοητὸς ὁ τῆς ἁμαρτίας (shortly before: ὁ τῆς ἁμαρτίας καὶ τῆς τότε κολάσεως).

τῇ καιομένῃ πυρὶ καὶ θείῳ). Although such torments are elsewhere thought of as the actual judgement of death they are nowhere depicted in the sense of Jewish or 'Orphic' ideas of the underworld. The essential curse of death is, at all events, destruction just as φθορά and ἀπώλεια characterise this end.[1]

What is more important is that the annihilating power of death is seen as already holding sway over life and destroying its essential nature (cf. p. 60). Impending death keeps life in φόβος (Heb. ii.15; Rom. viii.15) and those to whom Jesus is sent are considered καθήμενοι ἐν χώρᾳ καὶ σκιᾷ θανάτου (Matt. iv.16; Luke i.79 following Isa. ix.1 f.). Life, indeed, is always a life 'unto . . .' (cf. p. 60), 'unto God' or 'unto death' (Rom. vi.13-23). Only of the believer is it true that he lives and dies unto the Lord (Rom. xiv.7). But what all flesh is intent upon in the last analysis is θάνατος (Rom. viii.6) so that if there were no hope to be established by Christ it would really be true to say: φάγωμεν καὶ πίωμεν αὔριον γὰρ ἀποθνήσομεν (I Cor. xv.32). The uncertainty of the morrow makes all anxiety senseless (Matt. vi.25-34); no-one knows whether he will be alive tomorrow (Luke xii.16-21). Just as at the back of hope and care, so also at the back of the λύπη of the κόσμος stands death (II Cor. vii.10) and all the works of man are νεκρά from the beginning (Heb. ix.14; cf. p. 60). Thus, in anticipation, men can already be described as νεκροί (Matt. viii.22 and parallels) especially since they are sinners,[2]

---

[1] φθορά, e.g. Gal. vi.8. ἀπώλεια, e.g. Phil. iii.19. Barn. xx.1 speaks of the ὁδός . . . θανάτου αἰωνίου μετὰ τιμωρίας, ἐν ᾗ ἐστιν τὰ ἀπολλύντα τὴν ψυχὴν αὐτῶν According to Herm. v. I.1.8 the wicked bring θάνατον καὶ αἰχμαλωτισμόν upon themselves.

[2] Rom. vi.11, 13; Col. ii.13; Eph. ii.1, 5, v.14. In contrast Luke xv.24, 32 has a metaphorical usage. For the use of νεκρός see p. 60, n. 6. When it is said in James ii.26: ὥσπερ γὰρ τὸ

so that in Rom. vii.10 Paul can simply say: (ἐλθούσης δὲ τῆς ἐντολῆς) ἡ ἁμαρτία ἀνέζησεν ἐγὼ δὲ ἀπεθάνον, just as he describes his σῶμα in vii.24 as a σῶμα του θανάτου, and so that in I John iii.14 it can be said of the pseudo-Christian who has no love that he 'abides in death'. Outside revelation men are simply dead people (John v.21, 25).

4. The destruction of death in Christ

Death, therefore, as an annihilating force stands over the life of men and is inescapable outside revelation. In revelation, however, i.e. through Christ, God has destroyed death (II Tim. i.10; Heb. ii.14; cf. p. 63). Indeed Christ's death and resurrection are the eschatological event. His death was not a normal human fate but the death which God caused him to die for us. He did not deserve his death by his sin but was made a sinner for us by God and condemned as one (II Cor. v.21; Rom. viii.3; Gal. iii.13 f.); he died for us.[1] The

σῶμα χωρὶς πνεύματος νεκρόν ἐστιν this is derived from a naive dualistic anthropology. If the power of vitality does not fill the σῶμα it is dead. In contrast it is seen in a Hellenistic dualistic sense when Ign. Sm. v.2 says of men that they are νεκροφόρος (cf. p. 56, n. 1). Therefore Ignatius can also ask the Romans (vi.2): μὴ ἐμποδίσητέ μοι ζῆσαι, μὴ θελήσητέ με ἀποθανεῖν (they must not prevent his martyrdom). Also Hellenistic terminology is in the background when Dg. x.7. contrasts δοκῶν ἐνθάδε θάνατος with ὄντως θάνατος.

[1] Christ's death ὑπὲρ ἀσεβῶν: Rom. v.6. ὑπὲρ ἡμῶν (ὑμῶν): Rom. v.8 (I Cor. i.13, xi.24); II Cor. v.21; Gal. iii.13; Eph. v.2; Titus ii.14; I Peter (ii.21), iv.1; I John iii.16; Ign. Rom. vi.1; Ign. Pol. ix.2. ὑπὲρ ἐμοῦ: Gal. ii.20 (cf. Rom. xiv.15). ὑπὲρ πολλῶν: Mk. xiv.24 (cf. x.45). ὑπὲρ ἀδίκων: I Peter iii.18. ὑπὲρ παντῶν: Rom. viii.32; II Cor. v.14 f.; I Tim. ii.6 (cf. Heb. ii.9). ὑπὲρ αὐτῆς (τῆς ἐκκλησίας): Eph. v.25 (cf. Col. i.24). ὑπὲρ (τῶν) ἁμαρτιῶν (ἡμῶν): I Cor. xv.3; Gal. i.4; Heb. x.12 (cf. I Peter iii.18: περὶ ἁμαρτιῶν). Different phrases with ὑπέρ: John vi.51, x.11, 15; xi.51 f., xv.13, xvii.19, xviii.14. Formal piling up of

question as to how far the ideas of an expiatory sacrifice, or of substitution, or how far the concepts from the mysteries are dominant in such passages, can be left undecided (see commentaries on the relevant passages). The prevailing idea is that, in Christ, God was dealing with the world (II Cor. v.19) and that in such action by God Christ was taking death upon himself and thus death has lost its destructive character and taken on the creative character of divine action. Thus in his death resurrection is established. This act of dying has finished with sin [1] and thus with death; out of it grew life. As Christ was dead so he became alive (Rom. viii.34, xiv.9; I Thess. iv.14); death could not hold him (Acts. ii.24); he now has the keys of death and Hades (Rev. i.18). Just as he gave his life freely so he takes it again (John x.18). Because he humbled himself to the death of the cross God has exalted him (Phil. ii. 6-11). For those who appropriate his death to themselves in faith their own death is thereby also overcome so that Christ can be called πρωτότοκος (ἐκ) τῶν νεκρῶν (Col. i.18; Rev. i.5; cf. Rom. viii.29).

such phrases, Dg. ix.2. Corresponding phrases with περί (often with the variant reading ὑπέρ): Matt. xxvi.28; Rom. viii.3; I Thess. v.10; I Peter iii.18; I John ii.2, iv.10. Phrases with διά: Rom. iii.25, iv.25; I Cor. viii.11; II Cor. viii.9 (I Peter i.20); Ign. Tr. ii.1. Other descriptions of the saving significance of the death of Christ: Rom. iii.24; Col. i.20-22, ii.13 f., etc. Cf. Barn. v.6, vii.2 (ἵνα ἡ πληγὴ αὐτοῦ ζωοποιήσῃ ἡμᾶς) and the variations of the theme in Ignatius: Mg. ix.1; Tr. ii.1 f., ix.1 f.; Phld. viii.2; also in Pol. i.2. If occasionally the death and resurrection of Christ are spoken of together as two separate events, nevertheless both belong together in the unity of one event. The division is only rhetorical as in Rom. iv.25 or it is used to emphasise the unity as in Rom. v.10, viii.32-35.

[1] Rom. vi.7-10, viii.3. For the formulae corresponding to the Jewish principle of the law see Str.-B. III, p. 323 (on Rom. vi.7), p. 234 (on Rom. vii.3). K. G. Kuhn, Rom. vi.7 ZNW 30 (1931), pp. 305 ff. H. Windisch, *Taufe und Sünde* (1908), p. 173.

Believers are still, it is true, subject to death as far as it is the physical act of dying. Only in the early days, when there was an imminent expectation of the parousia, is it held that this fate will not strike all (Mark ix.1; I Thess. iv.15; I Cor. xv.51 f.). In any case, the annihilation of death will be experienced either in the resurrection or in the transformation which will take place with the parousia. When the expected eschatological events have reached completion, there will be no more death (I Cor. xv.26; Rev. xxi.4). But at the same time dying has already lost its sting for the believer; he already has the victory (I Cor. xv.55). Just as impending death destroys the whole of life for the unbeliever, so also the impending resurrection gives the whole of life a new character in advance. Thus there are found in John the bold statements that the believer will not die (vi.50, xi.25 f.), that he has passed from death into life (v.24; I John iii.14; cf. p. 75). And Paul makes use of the Anthropos-myth to make explicit the actuality of ζωή (cf. p. 67). The possibility of this notion being misunderstood in the Gnostic sense as the certain possession of an immortal nature is obviously controverted not only by II Tim. ii.18 but already, in a certain way, by I Cor. xv. For the view of the Corinthians which Paul combats (misunderstanding them it is true) is obviously not that death is the end of everything (which is refuted by xv.29 in any case). Nor do they believe in a coming new life bestowed by the miracle of the resurrection. Rather they believe in a transformation of their nature which has already taken place, as, of course, Gnostic ideas as a whole threaten to poison the church.[1] For faith, however, the annihilation of death is a present fact in ἐλπίς.[2] This is founded on the Gospel so that it can be said

[1] See *Gnosis* (1952) in this series.
[2] See *Hope* (1963) in this series.

quite simply that in the proclamation of the Gospel ζωή is present and death is destroyed (II Tim. i.10). Such ἐλπίς belongs organically to πίστις [1] and here the new life is a present fact (cf. p. 68). This means, however, that the destruction of death takes place not as it were, over and above the believers but in their believing obedience. As this means being taken up into the ζωή of Christ, part of it is also the assumption of the death of Christ, of the cross. The believer has died with Christ.[2] By using concepts from the mysteries Paul can express this in such a way that he describes baptism as a baptism into Christ's death and as being buried with him (Rom. vi.3 f.; cf. II Tim. ii.11), as a growing together with him.[3] How little he keeps to the ideas of the mysteries is, of course, shown by the change of image (Rom. vi.6): ὅτι ὁ παλαιὸς ἡμῶν ἄνθρωπος, συνεσταυρώθη, ἵνα καταργηθῇ τὸ σῶμα τῆς ἁμαρτίας, τοῦ μηκέτι δουλεύειν ἡμᾶς τῇ ἁμαρτίᾳ, i.e. the assumption

---

[1] See *Faith* (1961) in this series.

[2] Rom. vi.8 has ἀποθνῄσκειν σὺν χριστῷ; Col. ii.20 also has this sense. Also II Tim. ii.11: συναποθνῄσκειν and Rom. vi.6; Gal. ii.19: συσταυρωθῆναι. This is completely different from the συναποθνῄσκειν of the erotic friendship of men, married love and faithful discipleship which is dealt with by R. Hirzel, ARW 11(1908), p. 79, n. 1, which Fr. Olivier, Συναποθνῄσκειν (1929) in fact wants to use to explain ἀποθνῄσκειν σὺν χριστῷ. But the 'dying with' of a disciple in Mark xiv.31 and parallels, John xi.16 and of that of a friend in II Cor. vii.3 is only a matter of non-technical usage.

[3] Rom. vi.5: εἰ γὰρ σύμφυτοι γεγόναμεν τῷ ὁμοιώματι τοῦ θανάτου αὐτοῦ. The likeness (ὁμοίωμα) of his death is baptism. Τῷ ὁμοιώματι either depends on σύμφυτοι, then the shortened expression is used: *we have grown together in the ὁμοίωμα of his death,* i.e. baptism, or else σύμφυτοι must be supplemented with αὐτῷ then τῷ ὁμοιώματι is a dative of instrument. Cf. in addition to the commentaries, F. Blass, *Grammatik des ntl. Griechisch,* ed. A. Debrunner, (⁶1931), §194, 2; W. Schauf, *Sarx* (*Neutestamentliche Abhandlungen* XI 1/2, 1924), p. 48, n. 1; K. Mittring, *Heilswirklichkeit bei Paulus* (1929), pp. 75 f.

of death takes place in a new mode of life. This must be assumed in conscious decision (Rom. vi. 11): οὕτως καὶ ὑμεῖς λογίζεσθε ἑαυτοὺς εἶναι νεκροὺς μὲν τῇ ἁμαρτιᾳ, ζῶντας δὲ τῷ θεῷ ἐν χριστῷ Ἰησοῦ (cf. verse 2); and must be carried out in ὑπακοή under God or the δικαιοσύνη of those who are ἐκ νεκρῶν ζῶντες (Rom. vi.12 ff.).

The destruction of sin and death, which has taken place through Christ, must manifest itself in a mode of life which fulfils the Law's demands of justice (Rom. viii.2-4), in which being dead to sin (Rom. viii.10) takes place in a mortification of the πράξεις τοῦ σώματος (Rom. viii.13), in a καρποφορεῖν τῷ Θεῷ and δουλεύειν ἐν καινότητι πνεύματος (Rom. vii.4-6). Christ's death and resurrection receive their meaning for the believer in the fact that he no longer lives to himself but that his life and death are in the service of the κύριος (Rom. xiv.7-9). Christ has died for all and that means at the same time that all have died with him, ἵνα μηκέτι ἑαυτοις ζῶσιν, ἀλλὰ τῷ ὑπὲρ αὐτῶν ἀποθανόντι καὶ ἐγερθέντι (II Cor. v.14 f.; cf. Rom. xv.1-3). The leaving behind of the 'old man' must take place, γινώσκειν κατὰ σάρκα being excluded (II Cor. v.16 f.). The acceptance of the cross is realised in the life of faith (Gal. ii.19 f.) in this way, that in the cross of Christ the 'world' is crucified to the believer and he to the 'world' (Gal. vi.14).[1] If the communal celebration of the Lord's Supper proclaims the death of the κύριος (I Cor. xi.26), then the life of the believer has to take the matter seriously by worthy behaviour (I Cor. xi.27 ff.) and to sweep out the old leaven (I Cor. v.7 f.). His death has made us 'children of the day' who have so to walk (I Thess. v.5-10).[2] But this

---

[1] Imitated in Ign. Rom. vii.2: ὁ ἐμὸς ἔρως ἐσταύρωται.

[2] cf. also Col. i.22 f., iii.5; Eph. v.2, 25 f.; Titus ii.12; I Peter iv.1 f.; John xvii.19; I John iii.16.

new life does not have the conquest merely as an aim but rather it is present in it, for the desire to attain something by one's own effort is the very thing that has been done away with. With Christ's death the Law is abolished and every καύχησις excluded (Rom. iii.27). It is precisely this which is part of taking up the cross, to know that the Law has been done away with (Rom. vii.1-6; Gal. iii.13). To set up the Law again, to which, the believer has died (Rom. vii.6; Gal. ii.19; Col. ii.20), would nullify the death of Christ (Gal. ii.19-21). Participation in his death takes place in always being on the move, a state that never knows it has reached its goal but which always looks forward (Phil. iii.9-14).

Just as the taking on of Christ's death comes about in such a way that the believer lives to the Lord and thus for others, it does so also in that, in the fellowship of Christ, he sees the sufferings that come upon him in a new way; i.e. takes on these also as the cross, as the νέκρωσις τοῦ 'Ιησοῦ. That death is overcome is shown precisely in that διὰ 'Ιησοῦν he gives himself up daily to death and that such surrender to death leads to life for others in that he brings the proclamation of the Gospel to them.[1] Thus the sufferings of the apostle become simply a completion of Christ's sufferings (Col. i.24). The idea of unity with Christ in suffering must be the basis of the simple exhortation to obedience given by slaves (I Peter ii.8-21) just as much as the exhortation to bravery in persecution (I Peter iii.13–18). The idea of this unity is likewise a consolation. Believers who die are νεκροὶ ἐν χριστῷ (I Thess. iv.16; cf. v.14; I Cor. xv.18) especially martyrs (Rev. xiv.13) and the death of the Apostle is an ἀποθνήσκειν ὑπὲρ τοῦ ὀνόματος τοῦ κυρίου 'Ιησοῦ (Acts

---

[1] II Cor. iv.7-12, vi.9, xi.23, cf. Rom. viii.36; I Cor. xv.31: καθ' ἡμέραν ἀποθνήσκειν which is completely different from the 'cotidie mori' of Seneca.

xxi.31).[1] In death one glorifies God (John xxi.19). The same idea recurs in a different and more basic formulation in John xiii.31 ff., xv.11-14, where the commandment to love one another is based on the experience of the love of Jesus, the love which led him to death (cf. xiii.1).

Ζωή is understood in the idealistic sense as little as θάνατος. The new life mentioned above, and this new understanding of suffering and death, is not simply the conquest of death as an attitude of mind, but rather this assumption of the death of Jesus (just as it is not the grasping of an idea of Christ but attachment to a historical event) is an unfinished historical movement which is only conquest of death because it is moving forward to completion. We have died, it is true, but our ζωή is still hidden (Col. iii.3). For this reason there can grow out of the temporary nature of the present life the desire, like that for the parousia, for bodily death also which takes us out of this provisional state (II Cor. v.1-8; Phil. i.21-23; iii.9-14; cf. Rom. viii.18-30; Phil. iii.20 f.),[2] a longing which, it must be said, is limited in that the temporary life is positively seen as a service for the Lord (II Cor. v.9; Phil. i.24), though at the same time in the knowledge that τὸ ἀποθανεῖν κέρδος (Phil. i.21). In this sense death and life are made relative (Rom. viii.38; I Cor. iii.22).

If the act of salvation has destroyed death it has of course made it irrevocable for the ἀπολλύμενοι. For them the Gospel spreads nothing other than death (II Cor. ii.16, iv.3 f.; Phil. i.28; I Cor. i.18). They remain in death (I John iii.14; cf. John iii.36, ix.41, xv.22).

[1] In Ignatius this idea is expressed by: ἀποθνῄσκειν εἰς Ἰησοῦν χριστόν (Rom. vi.1 variant: ἐν, διὰ) and: εἰς τὸ αὐτοῦ πάθος (Mg. v.2) or ὑπὲρ θεοῦ (Rom. iv.1).

[2] In Ignatius it is even increased into a longing for martyrdom: Rom. vi.1: καλόν μοι ἀποθανεῖν εἰς χριστόν, vii. 2: ἐρῶν τοῦ ἀποθανεῖν.

ADDITIONAL NOTE TO CHAPTER V

1. θανατόω

θανατοῦν is an old word taken over from the Attic.[1] It means *to kill, to deliver up to death, to condemn to death*. In the sense of *kill* it is used in the LXX for *hēmīt* and *hārag*, e.g. Exod. xxi.12 ff.; I Macc. i.57. It is used of God in I Sam. ii.6; II Kings v.7 (cf. pp. 82, 83). In Josephus the word does not occur, but Philo uses it. In the NT θανατοῦν means *to kill* (human beings as the object of the verb) (Mark xiii.12 and parallels; II Cor. vi.9; also in Barn. xii.2; I Clem. xii.2; Dg. v.12).[2] Hyperbolically *to be given up to deadly peril* in Rom. viii.36 (following Ps. xliv.22 [LXX xliii.23]). Of Christ in I Peter iii.18 θανατωθ‿ις μὲν σαρκὶ, ζωοποιηθεὶς δὲ πνεύματι.[3] In that the believers participate in Christ's death (cf. p. 96), it can be said of them καὶ ὑμεῖς ἐθανατώθητε τῷ νόμῳ διὰ τοῦ σώματος τοῦ χριστοῦ: Rom. vii.4. θανατοῦν means 'to condemn to death' in Mark xiv.55 and parallels; Matt. xxvii.1.

θανατοῦν is frequently used by Philo in the figurative sense [4] and in the same way also Rom. viii.13 εἰ δὲ πνεύματι τὰς πράξεις τοῦ σώματος θανατοῦτε, ζήσεσθε. The figurative usage also in I Clem. xxxix.7 (following Job v.2 πεπλανημένον δὲ θανατοῖ ζῆλος) Herm. m. XII.1.3. ἐν ποίοις ἔργοις θανατοῖ ἡ ἐπιθυμία ἡ πονηρὰ τοὺς δούλους τοῦ θεοῦ,[5] further m. XII.2.2. and of vices s. IX.20.4.

[1] W. Schmid, *Der Attizismus* I (1887), p. 384, IV (1896), pp. 251, 651.

[2] Often in Justin, e.g. *Apol.* I.60.2; *Dial.* 39.6; 46.7. θανατώδη of the ἑρπετά Herm. s. IX.1.9 (variant θανάσιμα).

[3] Applied to the death of Christ also in Just. *Dial.* 94.2; 99.3; 102.2.

[4] *Leg. All.* II.87 (of the ἡδοναί). *Fug.* 53 ff. (allegorical explanation of θανάτῳ θανατούσθω: Exod. xxi.12-14).

[5] Also θανατώδεις of the ἐπιθυμίαι: Herm. m. XII.2.3.

2. θνητός

θνητός means *mortal*, used in Greek traditionally to characterise man so that the θνητοί are men, as opposed to the gods who are ἀθάνατοι.[1] Likewise in the LXX in characteristic instances: Job xxx.23 οἰκία γὰρ παντὶ θνητῷ γῆ (lᵉkol-ḥāy). Prov. iii.13 (for 'ādām in parallelism with ἄνθρωπος). Wisd. ix.14 λογισμοὶ γὰρ θνητῶν δειλοί.[2] Josephus uses θνητός to mean mortal (*Bell*. 6.84). he speaks of the θνητὴ φύσις (*Bell*. 7.345, *Ant*. 19.345) and describes the σῶμα as θνητόν (*Bell*. 3.372, 7.344).[3] The use of the word in Philo is very rich. He uses θνητός as an attribute of ἀνήρ (*Cher*. 43) and of ἄνθρωπος (*Op. Mund*. 77, *Spec. Leg*. 4.14), man is ὁ θνητός (*Sacr. A.C*. 76, *Mut. Nom*. 181, etc. Plural in *Leg. All*. 1.5.18, 2.80, etc.). Man as αἰσθητὸς ἄνθρωπος is according to Philo φύσει θνητός (*Op. Mund*. 134) but since he receives the divine πνεῦμα he stands between the θνητή and the ἀθάνατος φύσις.[4]

Paul uses θνητός as a necessary characterisation of human nature in I Cor. xv.53 f. δεῖ γὰρ το φθαρτὸν τοῦτο ἐνδύσασθαι ἀφθαρσίαν καὶ τὸ θνητὸν τοῦτο ἐνδύσασθαι ἀθανασίαν. He longs to be clothed with the heavenly body ἵνα καταποθῇ τὸ θνητὸν ὑπὸ τῆς ζωῆς (II Cor. v.4). He describes especially the σάρξ or the σῶμα (as do

---

[1] Hence the warning to remember that man is θνητός, in Epict. *Diss*. III.24.4; IV.1.95, 104. M. Ant. 4.3; 8.44.

[2] If Σ at Gen. ii.17 reads θνητὸς ἔσῃ instead of θανάτῳ ἀποθανεῖσθε (for mōt tāmōt) it is a correction (corresponding to the usual exegesis): not death but mortality is the consequence of eating the forbidden fruit.

[3] cf. Ecclus. ix.15: φθαρτὸν σῶμα.

[4] θνητός as an attribute of φύσις also in *Det. Pot. Ins*. 87; *Deus. Imm*. 77 et al. Concerning ζωή *Fug*. 39.59 et al.; concerning βίος *Op. Mund*. 152; *Leg. All*. II.57 et al.; concerning γένος *Op. Mund*. 61.135 et al.; concerning δόγμα *Leg. All*. III.35; concerning δόξα *Deus Imm*. 120; concerning ἔννοια *Det. Pot. Ins*. 87; concerning νοῦς *Op. Mund*. 165; concerning σῶμα *Mut. Nom*. 36. 187 et al.

Philo and Josephus) as θνητόν in II Cor. iv.11; Rom.
vi.12, viii.11.

In the Apostolic Fathers also one meets θνητός as a
characteristic attribute of man. Thus I Clem. xxxix.2
τί γὰρ δύναται θνητός; ἢ τίς ἰσχὺς γηγενοῦς. According to
Dg. ix.2 God gave up his son τὸν ἄφθαρτον ὑπὲρ τῶν
φθαρτῶν, τὸν ἀθάνατον ὑπὲρ τῶν θνητῶν. Dg. vi.8
describes the body as θνητὸν σκήνωμα. Human thinking
is called in vii.1 θνητὴ ἐπίνοια (parallel to ἐπίγειος and
ἀνθρώπινος). In Did. iv.8 the whole sphere of the
earthly is described as θνήτον, εἰ γὰρ ἐν τῷ ἀθανάτῳ
κοινωνοί ἐστε, πόσῳ μᾶλλον ἐν τοῖς θνητοῖς. Likewise
in the Apologists θνητός is a characteristic of human
nature (Aristides Apol. xi.6. Athenagoras Suppl. 28.4)
a characteristic which according to their polemical
writings is also peculiar to the heathen gods (Tatian
21.2. Athenagoras Suppl. 21.3). Man and his ψυχή
respectively are mortal because God's πνεῦμα has
separated itself from him (Tatian 7.3, 8.1, 13.1).
Christ has appeared as θνητός in his πρώτη παρουσία
(Just. Dial. 14.8).

3. ἀθανασία (ἀθάνατος)

1. Ἀθανασία, a word found in Greek since the time
of Philo and Isocrates and belonging essentially to the
literary language,[1] means immortality. According to
Greek belief this befits the gods, the ἀθάνατοι. Whether
it also describes human souls is a matter for discussion.
Plato attempts to 'prove' this [2] and among his disciples
the thesis of immortality becomes the characteristic
dogma [3] so that later Christian apologists refer to Plato

---

[1] T. Nägeli, Der Wortschatz des Apostels Paulus (1905), p. 18.
[2] cf. p. 30 f. Plato Phaedr. 246a.
[3] Max. Tyr. Diss. 41.5, p. 482. 19 f. (H. Hobein). Plotinus also
(Enn. IV.7) deals περὶ ἀθανασίας ψυχῆς.

and assert he has taken his doctrine from Moses.[1] In Hellenism the desire for immortality is strong but the belief in it is weak.[2] Apart from the διὰ τῆς δόξης ἀθανατισμός,[3] the attempt is made partly to find reassurance in the Stoic and pantheistic speculation that the individual belongs originally to the living cosmos and possesses in it an immortality though, however, not an individual one.[4] And partly the attempt is made to gain ἀθανασία through mysteries,[5] magic[6] or mystic vision.[7]

Such ἀθανασία is, of course, not thought of as mere duration but as participation in the blessed divine

---

[1] Just, Apol. I.44.9.

[2] cf. M. Ant. 4.48.

[3] Diod. S. I. 1.5, p. 3. 22 f. (F. Vogel), cf. ibid. I.2.4.

[4] Rohde II.310 ff. and cf. the pantheistic passages in Corp. Herm. VIII.3 treats of the ἀθανασία of the κόσμος as a ζῷον ἀθάνατον. Cf. also XII.15 ff.; XIV.10.

[5] On the old Greek and Orphic mysteries, Rohde I.278 ff., II.103 ff. G. Anrich, Das antike Mysterienwesen (1894), pp. 6 ff. W. Kroll, RGG IV.585 ff. H. Leisegang, RGG² IV.326 ff. O. Kern, ibid. 789 ff. On the mystery cults of the Hellenistic period Anrich, op. cit., pp. 34 ff. Leisegang, loc. cit. F. Cumont, Die orientalischen Religionen im röm. Heidentum (1931); ibid. on the longing for and faith in immortality, pp. 36 ff. et passim. Reitzenstein, Hell. Myst. passim, esp. pp. 102, n. 3; 222, 253 (also JHSt 4 (1883), pp. 419-421). As an example especially Apul. Met. XI.21.

[6] Reitzenstein op. cit. passim esp. pp. 169 ff., 185 ff. Th. Schermann, Griech. Zauberpapyri (TU 34,2b (1909)), pp. 40-44. The section of the Great Paris Spell-Papyrus (K. Preisendanz, Papyri Graecae Magicae (1928 ff.) IV.475-722 (834)) discussed by A. Dieterich under the title Eine Mithrasliturgie (1910, ³1923) is an ἀπαθανατισμός (Dieterich, p. 16, line 15), the initiate is promised ἀθανασία (p. 3, line 3, cf. 4.7 ff., 18 ff., 10.4 ff., 12.2 ff.: ἀπαθανατισθείς).

[7] Mithrasliturgie 4.10.18. The vision which leads to immortality is connected with speculation and asceticism in the dualistic passages in Corp. Herm. I.20, 28. Cf. also IV.5; X.4; XI.20; XIII.13. Ascl. 12.22 (Scott I.308, 20 f. 336, 9 ff.) also 27-29 (Scott I.364 and 370).

being, as deification.¹ Thus, in so far as something superhuman and divine can be discerned in a man, this can also be described as 'immortal'. According to Vett. Val. the capacity to foresee the future manifests a μέρος ἀθανασίας (p. 221.24, Kroll), an ἀπόρροια καιρικὴ ἀθανασίας (p. 330.20, cf. 242.16; 346.19 f.). This use is particularly strong in the cult of the monarch. The judgement of Antiochus I concerning Commagene is an ἀθάνατος κρίσις (Ditt. Or. I.383, 207). The divine majesty of the emperor (Gaius) is called μεγαλείου τῆς ἀθανασίας (Ditt. Syll.³ 798.5), his favour is ἀθάνατος χαρίς (ibid. 7 ff.). Thus everything that is spiritual can be described as ἀθάνατος. Where Paul, in Rom. xv.27; I Cor. ix.11 uses πνευματικός, the Didache iv.8 (cf. p. 102) uses ἀθάνατος. The Christian γνῶσις is called ἀθάνατος in I Clem. xxxvi.2.² On a papyrus of the 5th century, holy scripture is described as καλλίνικος καὶ ἀθάνατος (Preisigke, Sammelbuch 5273, 8), in Papyrus Oxyrynchus 1.130.21 (6th century) we meet ὕμνοι ἀθάνατοι.

The old notion that there is a food of immortality ³ plays a prominent part in the legend of a φάρμακον ἀθανασίας (or ζωῆς). According to the legend Isis is

¹ For ἀποθεωθῆναι cf. Reitzenstein op. cit., pp. 221 f. The magic action gives ἰσόθεος φύσις, Preisendanz, op. cit. IV.220.

² By contrast Wisd. i.15: δικαιοσύνη γὰρ ἀθάνατος ἐστιν means that the righteous are immortal. But probably Jos. Ant. 9.222 belongs here (Jeroboam χαυνωθεὶς (presumptuous) θνητῇ περιουσιᾷ τῆς ἀθανάτου ... ὠλιγώρησεν); 11.56 (all other heroes are θνητὰ καὶ ὠκύμορα (quickly passing away), the ἀλήθεια is ἀθάνατον χρῆμα καὶ αἴδιον), cf. IV Macc. vii.3 (‭‬).

³ H. Schlier, Religiongeschichtliche Untersuchungen zu den Ignatius-briefen (1929), p. 168, n. 1. Even the Greek legend knew a ἀθανατοποιὸν φάρμακον, E. Maass, ARW 21 (1922), p. 265. Mockingly Aristophanes Fr.86 (CAF): ὁ δὲ λιμός ἐστιν ἀθανασίας φαρμακον. According to Lucian Dial. Deorum 4.3.5 Ganymede is οὐκέτι ἄνθρωπος ἀλλ᾽ ἀθάνατος when he enjoys ambrosia and in nectar he drinks ἀθανασία.

said to have discovered this elixir and doctors also think they can dispense it.[1] The notion also plays a part in magic and mystery cults. According to the book of alchemy, called the 'Teaching of Queen Cleopatra', the φαρμάκον τῆς ζωῆς gives life to the dead.[2] The κόρη κόσμου (8, Scott, 1.463.13) speaks of ἱεραί βίβλοι who are (supplied?) with τῆς ἀφθαρσίας φάρμακον. The idea has penetrated even into the Jewish tradition. In a Jewish-Christian legend the angel says to Asenath, after he has offered her a honeycomb from paradise ἰδού δὴ ἔφαγες ἄρτον ζωῆς καὶ ποτήριον ἔπιες ἀθανασίας καὶ χρίσματι κέχρισαι ἀφαρσίας.[3] That the idea must have been familiar is shown by the new interpretation in Ecclus. vi.16: φίλος πιστός φάρμακον ζωῆς.[4] Ignatius to the Ephesians applies the term to the Christian Lord's Supper: xx.2. ἕνα ἄρτον κλῶντες ὅ ἐστιν φάρμακον ἀθανασίας, ἀντίδοτος[5] τοῦ μὴ ἀποθανεῖν, ἀλλα ζῆν ἐν Ἰησοῦ χριστῷ διὰ παντός.[6] So also Irenaeus in Contr. Haer. V.2.2 f. describes how the cup and the bread in the Lord's Supper incorporate the Logos and thus the ζωὴ αἰώνιος. In the Acts of Thomas 135 (M. Bounet, p. 242.1),

[1] cf. Diod. S. I.25, 6, p. 40, 23 f. Further in R. Reitzenstein, Hell. Wundererzählungen (1906), pp. 104-106; ARW 7 (1904), p. 402. Th. Schermann, Theol. Quartalschrift 92 (1910), pp. 6-19. W. Bauer on Ign. Eph. xx.2.

[2] Reitzenstein, Hell. Myst. 314.

[3] For more examples see E. Schürer, Geschichte III.400, 126.

[4] Hebrew reads ṣᵉrōr ḥāyyīm, which Smend translates by 'magic giving life' with reference to I Sam. xxv.29. (But cf. p. 36, n. 2.) The opposite is φάρμακον ὀλέθρου: Wisd. i.14 or θανάσιμον φάρμακον Ign. Tr. vi.2. Philo also knows the concept when in Fug. 199 he explains God, the πηγὴ τοῦ ζῆν (Jer. ii.13) as τὸ τῆς ἀθανασίας ποτόν.

[5] Also ἀντίδοτος is a technical term in medicine. Schermann loc. cit.

[6] Is the designation of Christ as the Physician connected with this?

also it is probably the Lord's Supper that is meant by the τῆς ζωῆς φαρμάκον. According to Irenaeus I.4.1 the Valentianians tell of how the Christ has left the fallen Achamoth an ὀδμή ἀφθαρσίας.

2. In so far as Judaism and Christianity have been influenced by syncretistic ideas they are discussed above. Concerning normal usage there is only a little to say. In the O.T. ἀθανασία has no equivalent. Only in the apocryphal writings of the LXX does ἀθανασία become the description of the expected eternal life of the righteous (Wisd. iii.4, xv.3; IV Macc. xiv.5),[1] just as also the ψυχή is characterised as ἀθάνατος in IV Macc. xiv.6, xviii.23 (cf. p. 51). 'Αθανασία, as also ἀθάνατος and (ἀπ) αθανατίζειν, is of course familiar to Philo.[2] Josephus in Bell. 7.340 records that Eleazar made a speech περὶ ψυχῆς ἀθανασίας and in Bell. 6.46 Titus speaks of the ἀθανασία of those fallen in battle.[3] Of the Essenes it is said in Ant. 18.18: ἀθανατίζουσι δὲ τὰς ψυχάς, and of the Pharisees in 18.14: ἀθάνατος ἰσχὺν ταῖς ψυχαῖς πίστις αὐτοῖς εἶναι.

3. In the N.T. ἀθάνατος does not occur. ἀθανασία is found only twice. In I Cor. xv.53 f., as in Hellenistic Judaism, the incorruptible mode of existence of the resurrected is called ἀφθαρσία and ἀθανασία. By this is meant not only eternal duration but also the mode of being in contrast to σάρξ and αἷμα, that which is elsewhere called δόξα (cf. p. 73) Besides this ἀθανασία is predicted of God in I Tim. vi.16: ὃ μόνος ἔχων

---

[1] Through the Greek translator, ἀθάνατος in the sense of immortal has entered the text of Ecclus. xvii.30, li.9 (A). Not very clear is the meaning of ἀθανασία in Wisd. viii.13, 17. In iv.1 ἀθανασία is the 'mnemonic' immortality, cf. p. 103, n. 3.

[2] cf. e.g. Virt. 9 and Leisegang, Index to Cohn and Wendland's edition of Philo's works.

[3] In the speech of Josephus, Bell. 3.372.

ἀθανασίαν in a context which shows the influence of Hellenistic Jewish terminology.[1]
Both uses found elsewhere. (On Did. iv.8 see p. 102.) In the Eucharistic prayer in the Didache (x.2) thanks are given ὑπὲρ τῆς γνώσεως καὶ πίστεως καὶ ἀθανασίας, ἧς ἐγνώρισας ἡμῖν διὰ Ἰησοῦ τοῦ παιδός σου (cf. ix.3. ὑπὲρ τῆς ζωῆς και γνώσεως).[2] In I Clem. xxxv.2 the first mentioned of the δῶρα of God is ζωὴ ἐν ἀθανασίᾳ and in II Clem. xix.3 consolation is given with the ἀθάνατος τῆς ἀναστάσεως καρπός in view.[3]

According to Athenagoras Suppl. 22.5 ἀθάνατον is the characteristic of the θεῖον (cf. 28.5). Dg. ix.2 describes Christ as ἀθάνατος. The Apologists treat of the ἀθανασία of the soul (cf. p. 62, n. 9). Dg. vi.8 calls it ἀθάνατος.

[1] cf. M. Dibelius, Pastoralbriefe (²1931), ad. loc.
[2] cf. further Th. Schermann, Griech. Zauberpapyri (cf. p. 103, n. 6), pp. 41-43.
[3] Ἀθανασία can also be used in the purely formal sense of everlasting continuation, so that it does not only count for the blessed (Just. Dial. 45.4; Tat. 20.3) but also for the damned (Tat. 13.1; 14.2).

INDEX OF REFERENCES

GENERAL INDEX